D1339617

Praise for

FOOD BABE
kitchen

"I love Vani! Her food industry investigations have made me a better
mother by opening my eyes to what's really going on and by making
me a healthier cook. We are paying attention to ingredients
more than ever, and it's because of her dedication to wellness on all levels.
The nutritious recipes, advice, and tips in *Food Babe Kitchen* are invaluable."

— **Eva Mendes**, actress, businesswoman, and mother of two

"I couldn't be more excited for Vani's first cookbook! I've been following her
for years as she's my go-to girl for all things health and wellness. Her passion
and perseverance have always been inspiring and now my family and I
love having her healthy and delicious recipes in our kitchen."

— **Kristin Cavallari**, founder and CEO of Uncommon James lifestyle brand,
two-time *New York Times* best-selling author of *Balancing in Heels*
and *True Roots*, and mother to three young kids

"If you want to be inspired, delighted, and overwhelmed with deliciousness look
no further than Vani Hari's masterful, yet simple everyday cookbook, *Food Babe Kitchen*.
Known for her fearless approach to telling the truth about what's really in our food, Vani
now provides a cornucopia of choices that start with real food, flavor, and healing;
and end with joy, happiness, and nourishment in every sense."

— **Mark Hyman, M.D.**, *New York Times* best-selling author of *Food Fix* and Head
of Strategy and Innovation at the Cleveland Clinic Center for Functional Medicine

"Vani is the matriarch of food transparency! Her deep knowledge and passion for
the quality of food available we eat are now combined with her love of feeding those
around her. What a gift to have the Food Babe sharing her tips, tricks for the types
of food we should be eating in over 100 delectable family-friendly recipes."

— **Catherine McCord**, cookbook author and founder of Weelicious

"Vani and I see eye to eye on nourishing our bodies with wholesome, real food meals made with high-quality, unprocessed ingredients. And this does not mean sacrificing taste . . . her recipes are delicious! My copy of *Food Babe Kitchen* is going to be well-worn with many pages flagged and splattered on."

— **Lisa Leake**, #1 *New York Times* best-selling author of *100 Days of Real Food*

"Vani sheds light on the processed food system and the negative impact chemicals, emulsifiers, and added sugars can have on each of us. Her new cookbook is an accessible tool I recommend to help clients stock a cleaner pantry, fridge, and freezer; and learn that simple homemade meals can be easy, clean, and delicious."

— **Kelly LeVeque**, celebrity nutritionist and best-selling author of *Body Love Every Day*

FOOD BABE
kitchen

ALSO BY VANI HARI

Feeding You Lies*

The Food Babe Way

*Available from Hay House

Please visit:

Hay House USA: www.hayhouse.com®
Hay House Australia: www.hayhouse.com.au
Hay House UK: www.hayhouse.co.uk
Hay House India: www.hayhouse.co.in

FOOD
BABE
kitchen

MORE THAN 100
Delicious, Real Food Recipes
to Change Your Body
and Your Life

VANI HARI

HAY HOUSE, INC.
Carlsbad, California • New York City
London • Sydney • New Delhi

Published in the United States by: Hay House, Inc.: www.hayhouse.com® • Published in Australia by: Hay House Australia Pty. Ltd.: www.hayhouse.com.au • Published in the United Kingdom by: Hay House UK, Ltd.: www.hayhouse.co.uk • Published in India by: Hay House Publishers India: www.hayhouse.co.in

Indexer: J S Editorial, LLC
Cover design: Shubhani Sarkar
Interior design: Julie Davison
Lifestyle photography by Susan Stripling
Recipe stylist and photography by Kim Ruggles
Sean Busher Photographer, page 85
Logos for Certified Animal Welfare Approved by AGW and Certified Grassfed by AGW are used with permission from A Greener World. Visit agreenerworld.org for a directory of certified farms and products.

Library of Congress Cataloging-in-Publication Data

Names: Hari, Vani, author.
Title: Food babe kitchen : more than 100 delicious, real food recipes to change your body and your life / Vani Hari.
Description: Carlsbad, California : Hay House, Inc., 2020. |
Identifiers: LCCN 2020026113 | ISBN 9781401960124 (hardback) | ISBN 9781401960131 (ebook)
Subjects: LCSH: Cooking (Natural foods) | Nutrition. | Health. | LCGFT: Cookbooks.
Classification: LCC TX741 .H37 2020 | DDC 641.3/02--dc23
LC record available at https://lccn.loc.gov/2020026113

Hardcover ISBN: 978-1-4019-6012-4
E-book ISBN: 978-1-4019-6013-1

10 9 8 7 6 5 4 3
1st edition, October 2020
Printed in the United States of America

SUSTAINABLE FORESTRY INITIATIVE
Certified Chain of Custody
Promoting Sustainable Forestry
www.sfiprogram.org
SFI-01268
SFI label applies to the text stock

*To my dear Harley,
may you always find joy spending time
in the kitchen and making nutritious
food with the best ingredients.*

CONTENTS

INTRODUCTION

Someone please pinch me, because I never imagined in my wildest dreams that I would become a cookbook author. As I write this introduction to *Food Babe Kitchen*, I am overwhelmed with feelings of nostalgia. Growing up, the kitchen was not a fun or friendly place. It was off-limits! No, seriously, my dad wanted good grades—not cooking skills—and he did whatever he could to keep me out of there. His overprotective anxiety started when I was really little. He would get nervous anytime I approached the oven or stove. As I got older, the only things I eventually figured out to make were in a microwave or cold out of the fridge.

Not having a foundation of cooking, even though my mother spent countless hours in the kitchen every day making food from scratch, is now so bizarre to think about. Right there in the kitchen of the house where I lived most of my life was a perfect example of how to cook. My mom was making food from the freshest ingredients, with the most amazing medicinal spices. When I was forced to tag along on her weekly trips to the farmers market, I hated going. Watching her pick vegetables and negotiate prices was not what I wanted to do. When we'd get home, she'd always ask me to shell the peas, which I did begrudgingly—but for some reason I never ate them. Once prepared, the dish looked so different from what all the other kids at school were eating. I didn't want that food. I wanted to be just like the kids around me.

Both of my parents are from northern India in Punjab and moved to the United States before I was born. Growing up in the U.S. allowed me to participate in two unique lifestyles. My parents made sure I was exposed to Indian culture, while also giving me the opportunity to choose a more American lifestyle when I wanted. I chose American food over Indian because I wanted to fit in. Often my mom would provide two separate meals for dinner: a traditional Indian dinner for my dad and an American take-out dinner for my brother and me. It wasn't until I got much older that I realized the value of that fresh Indian food. Missing out on it is one of the biggest regrets of my life.

When in high school, I quit the cheerleading team to join the debate team. That's where I learned how to research. I spent one summer at Wake Forest University and two summers at Dartmouth College at debate camp, spending countless hours in their law libraries and learning about various topics. I then spent 13 years of my adult life working as a management consultant at several

Fortune 500 companies. I was trained to help giant corporations quickly shift their policies, develop new strategies, and implement change within their organizations. This experience has allowed me to understand how the food industry works and how to make it change for the better. While a management consultant, I let my work life take over until I had my wake-up moment. Before that, I was either in the office eating whatever takeout was available, or I was on the road eating every meal out. Although this lifestyle allowed me to fit in with my peers and work crazy hours, it also took a huge toll on my body and I became very ill.

In 2002, I found myself in a hospital bed. I was sick, overweight, and ready to change! I made a personal promise to make my health my number one priority. When I started to research the food I was eating, I found that the majority of it was composed of man-made materials from a factory. I was not eating real food. The food was dead—which is how I felt most of my life. I didn't have energy, I had lots of health issues, I was on tons of prescription drugs, and I felt just like the food I was eating—*dead.*

I was walking around like a zombie and I knew the reason why: I was eating overly processed food filled with chemical additives. That realization grew into an insatiable curiosity about what I was eating, what was in it, and what caused me to feel this way. As I continued to research how food was made and what was actually in my food, I realized that I could no longer give up control to processed-food manufacturers. I had to figure out how to make food from living, real food ingredients, which is when I taught myself how to cook.

That is when everything changed in my life. All the health issues I had as a child—asthma, eczema, allergies—went away. I was on several prescription drugs at one time, but I'm on zero today. My weight normalized, and I began to have more energy than I had when I was years younger!

The way you treat yourself—the way you treat your body and what you put in it—can make a huge life-changing difference. Once I uncovered the truth about what was in my food, I knew I had to share that truth. Today, I'm known as the Food Babe (after the website I created, FoodBabe.com), and I've made it my mission to teach people to take a closer look at what they are eating, to read ingredient labels, know where their food comes from, and to demand transparency from the companies that are feeding the world.

> *I've made it my mission to teach people to take a closer look at what they are eating, to read ingredient labels, know where their food comes from, and to demand transparency from the companies that are feeding the world.*

Social media has helped me create a massive community of people who not only care about their own health but also want to create a safer, more sustainable food system for everyone. I lovingly call them the Food Babe Army. It is with their help that we have been able to force some of the largest food corporations to change for the better, including Kraft, Chick-fil-A, Chipotle, Subway, General Mills, Panera Bread, Anheuser-Busch, and Starbucks.

One of my biggest dreams was realized when I published my first book, *The Food Babe Way*, which debuted as a *New York Times* bestseller. The book contains the 21 essential habits that I taught myself to take control of my health. It is for anyone who is tired of the food industry hijacking their taste buds, and wants to take matters into their own hands and become their own food investigator, nutritionist, and food activist. I later followed this up with *Feeding You Lies*, a book that delves deep into the falsehoods we've been given about the food we eat—lies about nutrient value, effects on our health, label information, and even the very science on which we base our food choices.

Now that I'm a mom, I've been cooking more than ever. Teaching my daughter to make homemade meals from scratch is the biggest joy in my life. When I learned to cook in my 20s, Food Network and cooking shows were rising in popularity—and I'd binge-watch them every Saturday and Sunday to learn new recipes and techniques to use in my kitchen.

The hardest thing for me when I started cooking was how much time you had to spend in the kitchen. I wish I'd had an arsenal of recipes back then that were easy to make and didn't require hours of laboring. It took a few years of cooking mishaps, hours of cooking shows, and plenty of cookbooks to get to where I am today. But now I not only enjoy my time in the kitchen, I'm able to make delicious, unprocessed meals efficiently—and fast.

That is what I want to share with you in this cookbook. *Food Babe Kitchen* gathers together my favorite recipes, the things that I make for my own family every single week—and that they love—all in one place. It's a way for you to eat healthfully, close to the earth, with the best ingredients that you choose, so when you sit down to enjoy a delicious meal you know what you are eating and you haven't spent all day in the kitchen!

Cover Story

There's a porch just outside my kitchen where we grow vegetables. My husband has an incredible green thumb and takes requests every season to grow the plants we like to eat, in aboveground planters that we fill with organic soil and water with filtered water. Being able to just walk right outside and grab our own homegrown organic produce to make a salad is my dream come true. When we shot the cover of this cookbook, we had an array of the most delicious spicy arugula. It's so fresh and tastes amazing—even my daughter eats it. There's truly nothing better. It brings me so much joy to be able to share a glimpse of this happiness in my life with you.

PART I

CREATING YOUR FOOD BABE KITCHEN

chapter 1

SHOPPING FOR AND STOCKING THE BEST INGREDIENTS

Even if you don't make a single recipe from this cookbook, what I'm about to tell you is the most valuable information in this book. You see, cooking doesn't start with the recipe. It starts with the ingredients. What you use to make any meal is crucial to maintaining a healthy lifestyle. And dare I say, it's the only thing you should really concern yourself with when it comes down to how you decide to eat. In my best-selling book *Feeding You Lies*, I introduced readers to a very simple test I call the Three-Question Detox. All you need to do is ask yourself these three questions about any piece of food that passes your lips:

1. What are the ingredients?

2. Are these ingredients nutritious?

3. Where do these ingredients come from?

Easy, right? That's the beauty of this technique—it's so simple that anyone can do it. But let's go through this three-step process in detail. Pick up any product in your fridge or pantry and ask yourself these three questions:

QUESTION #1: WHAT ARE THE INGREDIENTS?

Flip the product over and find the ingredient list on the package. You can skip past the Nutrition Facts label, which tells you how many calories, carbs, or fat is in a serving. Simply scroll your eyes over to that list of ingredients and read it. Yes, the entire thing! If the ingredient list is long, that is typically the first indication that a product is heavily processed. If the food contains any additives (non-food ingredients) such as natural flavors, monosodium glutamate, or Red 40, you should question why they are used and whether they're really necessary. If you don't know what an ingredient or additive is or how it can affect your health, put the product down and look for an alternative.

Sticking to whole foods and a few packaged foods with simple ingredient lists will make this super easy for you. The fewer unnecessary ingredients added to your food, the better, and the more real whole foods you eat, the healthier your body will be. Choosing whole foods is the simplest way to answer this question without having any doubts because they contain only *one* ingredient. Examples include fresh fruits, fresh vegetables, nuts and seeds, legumes, and lean meats—all organic if possible.

QUESTION #2: ARE THESE INGREDIENTS NUTRITIOUS?

What kind of viable nutrition does your body get when you nosh on ingredients like Yellow 5, carrageenan, and natural flavors? The answer is *none*. Food additives have been created for the sole purpose of improving the bottom line of the food industry, not with our health or nutrition in mind. Food companies add these to their products to make them thicker, more colorful, and even to make their taste addicting so you keep coming back for more.

You may not immediately taste the difference between a product made with real raspberries versus artificial raspberry flavor, but your body will know the difference! The abundance of nutrients in real food are what your body thrives on, so make sure you are giving it what it needs. Instead of focusing on the calories, fat grams, or carbs, it's more important to emphasize the quality of those calories. Seek out nutrition first and the rest will follow.

QUESTION #3: WHERE DO THESE INGREDIENTS COME FROM?

Generally the food you buy has made a long journey before it makes it to your table, from grower to packer to distributor to supplier to the grocery store. Preservatives were probably used to extend shelf life and the food was likely cultivated with pesticides, chemicals, fertilizers, antibiotics, and growth hormones. Much of this information will not be found on the food's packaging, but if you are discerning, you can learn a lot about where your food came from. The USDA Organic label means that the United States Department of Agriculture has certified that no synthetic pesticides were used in the food's production and that it doesn't contain genetically modified (GMO) ingredients. It's best to avoid meat from animals raised on conventional factory farms, which are notorious for using hormones and other growth-promoting drugs, while feeding the animals antibiotics and GMO feed in cramped and unsanitary conditions. We will get more into how to know where your food comes from later in this chapter.

These three questions will tell you in a flash whether you should eat something (or not!). You can do this three-question detox just about anywhere. At the grocery store when you're shopping for pantry staples.

At the farmers market when you're picking up fresh local goodies. In your own kitchen when you're getting ready to cook a meal. And even when you're at a restaurant, although this can be more challenging, as they may refuse to tell you the ingredients in their food (they aren't legally required to). I say if they won't tell you what's in it, don't eat there! Find a restaurant that is transparent about its food and its practices. Follow this technique and you'll automatically feed your body with nourishing food from the earth and get healthier as a result.

So let's recap:

- Know what is in your food.
- Flip a product over to read the ingredient list.
- Ask yourself if those ingredients are good for you.
- Look for labels that have meaning, such as USDA Organic.

In the following pages, I will break this all down for you, aisle by aisle, product by product, so you can easily stock your kitchen the right way. Let's get started by cleaning the bad products out of your life so you can begin with a clean slate.

PURGE YOUR PANTRY!

When I first started my clean-eating journey, one of the best things I did was go through my cabinets and get rid of all the additive-filled junk. I donated it all and I haven't looked back. That includes things like baking powder with aluminum that I could have continued to use for another year or two. I made the decision that I could afford to do better.

It may seem like a waste of money to dispose of food that isn't expired, but I'd rather spend money on healthy food versus anything else. This is why I prefer to buy organic food to cook at home and why I eat at the best farm-to-table restaurants, which I know serve the highest-quality ingredients. This is why when I travel, I pack pricey travel-size foods including green powders, raw almond butter, and chia seeds. This is why it doesn't bother me to shop at the best natural-food grocery stores, even if their prices tend to be a bit higher than conventional stores. But this is also why I will save an eighth of an organic red onion. I am crazy about not wasting *good* food, too!

If your pantry is full of processed food, you're fighting an uphill battle with those temptations sitting in your cupboards. Boxes of instant potatoes and heat-and-eat meals are pretty tempting when you come home tired from work and want something quick. But we both know that your health is more important than that—which is why it is a big investment in your health to clean the processed junk from your pantry and kiss it good-bye, for good! So pick a lazy afternoon, grab a box, and get ready to set yourself up for success in the kitchen.

HEALTHY OR NOT? HOW TO DECIPHER TRICKY PRODUCT LABELS

Before you begin purging junk from your pantry, let's talk about food labels. If you've read any of my books, you'll know one thing: The ingredient label is the most important label on any product. That's where you'll find the truth about what is inside. However, the food industry knows most people don't read ingredient labels and instead are looking at the front of the packaging to see what they're buying. I hate to tell you this, but there are likely many products in your pantry that you thought were healthy when you bought them, because misleading labeling deceived you. You've heard of greenwashing, right? That's when a company makes its product appear more environmentally friendly than it really is. Well, the same thing happens to our food: It's called "health-washing."

Health-washing is when a food company adds synthetic and processed additives to make a product appear healthier and more nutrient-dense than it actually is. They'll add protein from heavily processed soybeans and slap a "10 Grams of Protein!" label on the front. Or they'll add synthetic vitamins made in a laboratory to a product so they can advertise that it's a "Great Source of Vitamins A and D!"—even though those nutrients don't come from the food itself and it's really just full of refined, bleached wheat and sugar. This is one of the dirtiest tricks in the book. And once you're aware of it, you'll start to see it everywhere in the grocery store.

Food companies will also add specific labels to their packaging to imply a product is healthy or will help you lose weight. Words like *diet, light, free, natural,* and *healthy* are put on packaging for foods filled with controversial additives that provide the body with zero nutrition. Remember, it pays to be wary of what it says on the front of a food package and not to take it at face value (go back to question number 1 in the Three-Question Detox and check that ingredient list to see if it's made with real food). Here are some common misleading labels you'll find on food products, and what these labels truly mean:

"All-Natural," "100% Natural," "Natural"

The U.S. Food and Drug Administration (FDA) does not have a very clear definition for what *natural* means on a label, so there is room for interpretation by food companies. This wording indicates that the product doesn't contain added colors or artificial ingredients.[1] However, this label absolutely does *not* mean that a product is organic, non-GMO, pesticide-free, preservative-free, humane, or made with real food. Many products say they are "100% Natural," even though they are full of unnecessary ingredients. Don't be duped!

"Fortified" or "Enriched"

When labels contain the words *fortified* or *enriched,* that's a red flag indicating an item is heavily processed. Both of these terms mean that nutrients have been added back into the product because its ingredients have been so overly processed that they've been stripped of nutritional value. For example, flour is refined and can be treated with dozens of different chemicals approved by the FDA— including bleach!—before it ends up on store shelves. This industrial processing destroys nutrients. So manufacturers will add nutrients back in, and often the nutrients and vitamins added back into the product are isolated and from synthetic sources. Synthetic nutrients are not always utilized as well by the body as the nutrients found naturally in whole foods are. It's better to choose foods that still contain their natural nutrients, rather than having been processed to the degree that they need to be "fortified" or "enriched."

"Multigrain"

The *multigrain* label is a bit of a mind trick. It sounds healthy, but probably doesn't mean what you think it does. If something is multigrain, it is made with multiple different types of grains.[2] This does not mean that these grains are whole and unrefined. Rather, these grains may be refined, and therefore stripped of their nutrients and healthy fiber.

"Made with Olive Oil" (or any other healthy ingredient)

This labeling trick by food companies is one of the sneakiest. Just because a product says on the front that it is "made with" something healthy doesn't mean that the rest of the ingredients are healthy too. A good example of this is Best Foods Mayonnaise Dressing with Olive Oil. You'd think it's made with healthy olive oil,

but a quick scan of the ingredient list will show you that it's actually made with more soybean oil than olive oil. Which begs the question, why don't they call it Best Foods Mayonnaise Dressing with Soybean Oil? Because that wouldn't increase sales now, would it?

"No Sugar Added" or "Sugar-Free"

How can a sugar-free product still taste sweet? By the use of fake sweeteners made in a lab, that's how. Many products labeled "sugar-free" contain artificial sweeteners such as aspartame and sucralose, which I would suggest avoiding.

"Fat-Free" or "Low-Fat"

This label is very misleading, as "fat-free" and "low-fat" products often contain more additives and more sugar than their original versions. This clearly doesn't make them more healthful! These products are packed with extra sweeteners along with added fillers and thickeners to replace the fat that was removed. This label also does not tell us anything about the quality of the ingredients or what was added to maintain the flavor after the fat was removed.

"Made with Real Fruit"

While the claim "made with real fruit" might lead you to imagine an abundant basket full of oranges, grapes, and strawberries, products with this label often contain very little fruit at all. Food companies aren't required to label the percentage of actual fruit in a product and so it might contain just one small cherry. This also goes for products that say they are made with "100% juice." For instance, Ocean Spray's 100% Juice Cranberry isn't just cranberry juice. It also contains grape juice, apple juice, natural flavors, pectin, and synthetic vitamin C. The company's website claims this juice contains one cup of fruit per serving.[3] But it may not be from one type, and since when did concentrated juices mixed with flavors and synthetic vitamins equate to real fruit?

"High in Protein"

Any product that boasts about how much protein it contains is often fortified with extra protein in the form of soy protein isolate or whey protein isolate, both of which are heavily processed forms of protein. Although you can take virtually any super-unhealthy product out there (like a sugary chocolate muffin made with corn syrup and refined flour) and add some protein powder to it, this does not magically transform it into a health food muffin. Many protein-fortified products are filled with refined sugar, fake flavors, and synthetic preservatives.

"Good Source of Fiber"

Just like they add protein to some products, food manufacturers will add fiber additives to processed products full of white flour and sugar to make them seem healthier. Often they'll include the additive cellulose to artificially pump up the fiber content. This additive is typically derived from wood, as cellulose is much cheaper to obtain from wood than fruits and vegetables, and is manipulated in a laboratory to form different structures (liquid, powder, etc.) depending upon the food product in which it's used. Cellulose may be a cheap way to boost the fiber content on food labels, but it isn't as healthful as the fiber you get from eating whole grains or produce. Research links the additive cellulose to increased risk of weight gain, inflammation, and digestive problems[4]—which is quite the opposite result than you'd expect from eating fiber-rich foods, right? It's best to get your fiber from whole grains, fruits, and veggies, instead.

The Ultimate "No-No" List

Did you know that the FDA hasn't reviewed the safety of thousands of food additives, and isn't aware that many of them exist?[5] Crazy, right? That means that possibly dozens of products sitting in your kitchen right now could be filled with questionable additives linked to all sorts of health issues. Many people assume that everything allowed into the food we are able to buy has been proven safe to eat and that the FDA is ensuring the safety of all ingredients in processed food. They also assume that if food additives are found to be dangerous to human health, they will be removed from the food supply. Sadly, that is not the reality.

This is why it's up to you to know what the specific ingredients are that you should watch out for on every label. The additives listed below are what I've identified as the most important ingredients to avoid in processed foods, because I have found they are associated with negative health issues. If a product contains any of the additives on this "No-No" List, try finding an alternative or make the food at home, from scratch.

- Acesulfame potassium
- Artificial flavors
- Aspartame (NutraSweet)
- Autolyzed yeast extract
- Azodicarbonamide
- BHA and BHT
- Bleached flour
- Blue 1
- Calcium peroxide
- Calcium propionate
- Caramel color
- Carrageenan
- Cellulose
- Corn syrup
- Cottonseed oil
- DATEM
- Dextrose
- Dimethylpolysiloxane
- Enriched flour
- Erythritol
- Fructose or fructose syrup
- High-fructose corn syrup
- Hydrolyzed proteins
- Maltodextrin
- Methylparaben
- Monoglycerides and diglycerides
- Monosodium glutamate (MSG)
- Natural flavors
- Neotame
- Potassium benzoate
- Partially hydrogenated oils
- Propyl gallate
- Propylparaben
- Red 3
- Red 40
- Sodium benzoate
- Sodium nitrate
- Sodium nitrite
- Sodium phosphate
- Soybean oil
- Soy protein isolate
- Sucralose (Splenda)
- Synthetic vitamins
- TBHQ
- Titanium dioxide
- Vanillin
- Yeast extract
- Yellow 5
- Yellow 6

HOW TO SHOP FOR THE HEALTHIEST FOOD

This chapter offers a step-by-step guide to help you navigate your way through any grocery store with ease. I'll take you through each major food category and outline what to look for on the package to find the healthiest options. I'll also explain why certain products are a poor choice for your health, and what would make a better choice.

The most important thing to remember when grocery shopping is that most of the food you buy should be one ingredient. Yes, only one. That means you should spend the vast majority of your time in the produce section, picking up fresh and flavorful fruits and vegetables. And then find your way into the center of the store to stock your pantry with all the ingredients that you'll need to cook healthy meals on the fly, such as quinoa, rice, olive oil, beans, etc. Once your pantry is stocked and you've got your fresh produce, dairy, and meats for the week, you will have the makings for success in the kitchen. Let's break down each aisle of the grocery store.

DAIRY

Milk: Milk that is not certified organic comes from cows likely raised on grains and GMO feed, which is not healthy for them and produces less nutritious milk. It also may contain residues of artificial growth hormones, antibiotics, and synthetic pesticides.

Organic milk comes from cows fed 100 percent organic feed and no GMOs or antibiotics. Additionally, dairy products from grass-fed cows have been shown to have an improved omega-6 to omega-3 fat ratio, higher levels of beneficial fats such as CLA (conjugated linoleic acid, a fatty acid that is good for you and associated with fat loss), and more antioxidants.[6]

Ideally, look for dairy labeled "100% Grassfed," which indicates that it's Certified Grassfed by AGW, American Grassfed Association Certified, or Certified Grassfed Organic Dairy:

Butter: Conventional nonorganic butter comes from cows fed almost entirely GMO corn and soy. The harmful pesticides used on conventional feed are being eaten by these cows and can end up in their milk[7]—and thereby, their butter.

Also, grass-fed cows produce butter with up to 50 percent more vitamin A and E and 400 percent more beta carotene (which gives the grass-fed butter a deeper yellow color).

Margarine: Most margarines are made with inflammatory oils such as soybean oil that are most surely GMO (unless specified otherwise). They also can contain hidden trans fat additives (including mono- and diglycerides), flavors, and artificial preservatives.

Skip all the fake butter spreads that contain GMO inflammatory oils such as soybean oil. Instead, choose real food like organic pastured butter, 100 percent coconut oil, olive oil, or hemp oil instead. Coconut butter works well too; when slightly heated it spreads just like butter.

Yogurt: Instead of using any real fruit, many yogurts contain natural or artificial flavors to make them taste like fruit. This may save on calories, but it's better to add real fruit to yogurt so that you get the nutrition. Artificial flavors are created in a laboratory and contain a long list of secret ingredients that are not disclosed on the label.

Choose yogurt made with organic milk, which comes from cows fed 100 percent organic feed and no GMOs. Ideally, look for yogurt labeled "100% Grassfed," which indicates that it's Certified Grassfed by AGW, American Grassfed Association Certified, or Certified Grassfed Organic Dairy.

Cheese: As with all dairy products, you'll want to stay away from cheese that comes from conventional cows. Most pre-shredded cheese in a bag contains powdered cellulose, an additive usually made from wood and used as a coating to keep the cheese from sticking together. Eating cellulose is linked to weight gain, inflammation, and digestive problems.

MILK

Poor choice:	Better choice:
* Not organic	* Certified organic
* Not grass-fed	* 100% grass-fed

BUTTER

Poor choice:	Better choice:
* Not organic	* Organic pastured butter
* Not grass-fed	

MARGARINE and SPREADS

Poor choice:	Better choice:
* Soybean oil	* Organic pastured butter
* Monoglycerides and diglycerides	* Coconut oil
* Natural flavors	* Coconut butter
* Not organic	* Olive oil
	* Hemp oil

YOGURT

Poor choice:	Better choice:
* Not organic	* Certified organic
* Not grass-fed	* Plain
* Added sugar	* No added flavors
* Artificial colors	* No added sweeteners
* Artificial sweeteners: acesulfame potassium, sucralose	* No thickeners or gums
* Added flavors instead of real fruit	

CHEESE

Poor choice:	Better choice:
* Not organic	* Certified organic
* Not 100% grass-fed	* 100% grass-fed
* Pre-shredded	* Raw
* Contains cellulose (wood)	* Whole block of cheese. Shred it yourself!

Choose organic, raw, 100 percent grass-fed cheese and shred it yourself with a grater. Raw cheese contains enzymes that make it easier to digest and is more nutritious. Goat milk cheese is also an excellent option that's easier to digest.

Eggs: The label "cage-free" on eggs means the chickens they come from weren't in a cage, but it doesn't mean they spent any time outside. These chickens likely lived crammed together inside large warehouses or barns, and may not have had any access to the outdoors. Eggs that aren't organic but vegetarian-fed were likely raised on GMO feed, and labels with words such as *natural* or *farm fresh* are just marketing tools.

Organic pastured eggs come from hens that forage naturally on a pasture, eating a natural diet of grass, bugs, worms, and perhaps organic supplemental feed (no GMO feed allowed). This produces more nutritious eggs with up to twice as much vitamin E and omega-3 fatty acids, and a healthier ratio of omega-6 to omega-3 fatty acids. Pasture-raised eggs that also carry the Certified Humane label are third-party certified that each hen has a minimum of 108 square feet of space outdoors year-round, on grassy fields, with fixed or mobile housing for sleeping and protection.

MEAT

Poultry: The terms *fresh, natural,* and *100% all natural* are not properly regulated and don't mean what they should, so don't rely on shady marketing tactics that use these words on food products. Another phrase that fools so many people is *no added hormones.* When you're shopping for chicken (or any type of poultry), remember that growth hormones are already banned from poultry production.[8] So there is no reason to put that on the label except marketing, as any poultry you purchase can make this claim.

Chickens that are humanely raised on pastures are healthier and more nutritious than their indoors-only counterparts, with higher levels of omega-3 fatty acids. Sadly, organic chickens can be raised in factory-farm conditions, so this label does not ensure they were raised much more humanely than conventional chickens. However, routine antibiotics and GMO ingredients are prohibited from their food, and they are fed only organic food. Organic chickens must also be given access to the outdoors.[9] The Animal Welfare Approved (AWA) label is an independent certification that the chicken comes from sustainable, pasture-based family farms. Ideally, look for the organic label along with the Animal Welfare Approved by AGW, or Certified Humane label.

Beef: Angus beef comes from a breed of cattle that has met some quality requirements, none specifying how the cows were raised. Likewise, the "natural" label on beef also doesn't specify how the cows were raised—only that the meat contains no artificial ingredients or added colors, and is minimally processed. Neither "Angus beef" nor "natural" on the label mean that the cows were grass-fed, organic, or humanely raised. The word *natural* itself does not indicate that no antibiotics or hormones were used; this would be indicated separately on the packaging.[10] The usual diet for cows is likely GMO grains and candy.[11]

"Free Range" beef is another meat-package label with little meaning. Free-range cows are required to have continuous access to the outdoors, but the regulations do not specify the size of the space or that there is vegetation growing in the space.[12] The USDA also does not verify this claim by conducting on-farm inspections, so the label is used too freely.

To earn the claim "100% Grassfed," cows are fed grass and forage that grows on the pasture during the growing season, and during the winter they're fed hay and compacted grass. This has a major effect on the nutrient composition of their meat. Grass-fed cows produce meat with significantly more omega-3 fatty acids and almost twice as much CLA. Their meat is also packed with more vitamins A and E than conventional beef.[13]

Cows' digestive systems are not designed to easily process starchy foods such as corn and candy, which can make conventional cows sick.[14] That's one reason why grass-fed cows are rarely given antibiotics: Because they are spending more time outdoors instead of a crowded, filthy feedlot, they are less likely to get sick. Sustainably raised grass-fed beef is also less likely to harbor deadly bacteria, such as *E. coli* and *Staphylococcus aureus* (a bacteria that produces a toxin that is not easily destroyed by cooking).[15]

Fish: When shopping for fish, you want to select those that are clearly labeled "wild" or "wild-caught." If it isn't labeled this way, then it is likely farm-raised. Farmed fish is less nutritious and can contain higher levels of toxins than fish in the wild.[16] For instance, farmed salmon often turn gray due to the poor diet they are given; they are fed fish supplements to dye their flesh pink so that it looks better at the store![17] No matter where they are raised, fish can also be a source of toxic heavy metals, such as mercury. That's why it's advised that you limit fish to once or twice a week and choose fish known to have lower levels of mercury (salmon, trout, haddock, pollock, and Atlantic mackerel).

EGGS

Poor choice:

* Not organic
* Not pastured
  ### Misleading labels:
  "Cage-Free"
  "Vegetarian Diet"
  "Natural" or "Naturally Raised"
  "No Hormones"
  "Farm Fresh"

Better choice:

* Certified organic
* Pastured
* Certified Humane

POULTRY

Poor choice:

* Not organic
* Not pastured
  ### Misleading labels:
  "Fresh"
  "Natural" and "100% All Natural"
  "No Added Hormones"

Better choice:

* Organic and pastured
* No antibiotics
* Animal Welfare Approved
* Certified Humane

BEEF

Poor choice:

* Not organic
* Not grass-fed
  ### Misleading labels:
  "Natural"
  "Angus"
  "Free Range"

Better choice:

* 100% grass-fed and finished
* Certified organic
* AWA Certified Grassfed or American Grassfed

FISH

Poor choice:

* Farm-raised
* Dyed
* Added preservatives
* High risk of mercury

Better choice:

* Wild-caught
* Low risk of mercury (low on food chain)

PANTRY ITEMS

Condiments: It's difficult to find healthy condiments at the store as almost every one (even organic) is made with either soybean oil or sunflower oil. These are refined and very high in omega-6 fatty acids, which leads to inflammation in the body. Many popular condiments also include added sugars, corn syrup, flavors, MSG, and artificial preservatives.

Look for certified organic condiments made with real food ingredients and only healthy oils such as extra-virgin olive oil, coconut oil, or avocado oil. Unfortunately most store-bought versions still contain sweeteners and other questionable oils which is not ideal, so try to avoid or minimize those ingredients.

Cooking Oils: Vegetable oils, including canola, soybean, and corn, go through an insane amount of processing with chemical solvents, steamers, neutralizers, dewaxers, bleach, and deodorizers before they end up in the bottle. The "solvent" most often used to extract the oil is the neurotoxin hexane—the raw material is literally bathed in it. These oils are also very high in omega-6 fatty acids, which fuel chronic inflammation in the body, leading to disease.

Choose unrefined, expeller-pressed organic oils. GMOs and hexane extraction are prohibited in organic oil production, so you can avoid those simply by choosing organic oils. The healthiest cooking oils include cold-pressed extra-virgin olive oil, coconut oil, avocado oil, hemp oil, and ghee. The tropical saturated fat in coconut oil is made up of medium-chain triglycerides (MCT), which have been shown to reduce cholesterol and obesity.

Sweeteners: Refined sugar (such as white sugar and corn syrup) has zero nutritional value. Eating refined sugar is addictive; it makes you fat, tired, depressed, and age faster; dulls your skin; weakens immunity; and when consumed in excess, causes all sorts of diseases. Unless a sugar says it is "cane sugar" it is probably made from GMO sugar beets. Any sugar (including cane sugar) that is *not* organic could have been sprayed with Roundup (glyphosate) weed killer pre-harvest.[18]

Most stevia sweetener products on the market are not pure stevia and contain mostly erythritol (a sugar alcohol made from corn). Truvia (Coca-Cola's branded stevia product) goes through about 40 steps to process the extract from the stevia leaf, relying on chemicals such as acetone, methanol, ethanol, acetonitrile, and isopropanol. Some of these chemicals are known carcinogens (substances that cause cancer).

Low-calorie artificial sweeteners such as Splenda, NutraSweet, Equal, and Sweet'N Low are also linked to health risks. Splenda (sucralose) is an artificial sweetener made by chlorinating sugar. Independent animal research links it to leukemia and other blood cancers.[19] NutraSweet and Equal (aspartame) are linked to increased risk of brain tumors, lymphomas, leukemia, and heart disease.[20]

Although they have no calories, artificial sweeteners have been shown to contribute to weight gain by encouraging sugar cravings. Research has found that these

COOKING OILS

Poor choice:

* Soybean oil
* Canola oil
* Corn oil
* "Vegetable oil"
* Not organic

Better choice:

* Organic
* Cold-pressed
* Pastured butter
* Extra-virgin olive oil
* Coconut oil
* Avocado oil
* Hemp oil
* Ghee

CONDIMENTS

Poor choice:

* Refined soybean, sunflower, or canola oils
* Added sugars
* Not organic
* Synthetic preservatives

Better choice:

* Real food ingredients
* Certified organic
* Extra-virgin olive oil, coconut oil, or avocado oil

SWEETENERS

Poor choice:

* Sugar
* Cane sugar
* Corn syrup
* Low-calorie sugar substitutes (Truvia, Splenda, Equal, Sweet'N Low)

Better choice:

* Raw honey
* Grade B maple syrup
* Coconut sugar
* Dried fruit (such as dates or raisins)
* Fresh fruit (such as bananas or mango)
* Monk fruit or *luo han guo*

PROTEIN POWDER

Poor Choice:

* Not organic
* Added flavors
* Added sugar
* Artificial sweeteners
* Sweetened with stevia
* Heavily processed proteins (such as soy or whey isolate)

Better Choice:

* Certified organic
* Made without isolated proteins
* No added sugar
* No added flavors
* No artificial sweeteners
* 100% real food, free of additives
* No gums or stabilizers

SPICES

Poor choice:

* Not organic
* Added ingredients
  (such as MSG or cellulose)

Better choice:

* Certified organic
* No additional ingredients
  (100% spices)

NUT BUTTER

Poor choice:

* Not organic
* Added sugar
* Added oil
* Roasted (not raw)

Better choice:

* Certified organic
* Raw
* One ingredient (nuts)

stimulate your appetite, increase sugar cravings, and promote fat storage and weight gain.[21] When you eat something sweet—even when it has no calories—your brain is tricked into wanting to eat more because your body is not getting enough energy (i.e., calories) to be satisfied. So you keep craving sweets, eating sweets, and gaining weight. This is why a lot of people never reach their full health potential or weight-loss goals, because they are constantly being pushed around by these chemical artificial sweeteners that trick the brain and body.

You can easily replace white sugar in any recipe with organic coconut sugar. It's a perfect 1 to 1 substitute for regular old sugar. Coconut sugar is completely unrefined and not bleached, which helps to preserve all of its vitamins and minerals. Other good natural sweeteners include raw honey, monk fruit or *luo han guo* or Grade B maple syrup.

Spices: Conventional (nonorganic) spices are often treated with chemicals and may contain GMO additives, cellulose, and pesticide residues. Virtually all conventional spices sold in the United States are fumigated (sterilized) with hazardous chemicals that are banned in Europe.

Some brands have their spices irradiated—a process of using radiation to kill bacteria and other contaminants—leaving the finished product with decreased levels of vitamins and natural enzymes. Irradiation also changes the chemical composition of a spice, potentially creating toxic, carcinogenic by-products and increasing our exposure to free radicals. Free radicals cause aging and disease.

Organic spices are never irradiated and cannot contain genetically engineered ingredients (GMOs), artificial colors, preservatives, or anticaking agents.

Protein Powder: It's common to find protein powders made with "isolated" proteins, such as soy protein isolate or whey protein isolate. When soy is isolated to just its protein state, it becomes severely denatured and can cause hormonal disruptions because of the excessive amount of estrogen it contains. Soy also contains an abundance of phytic acid, which leaches calcium and other vital minerals from your body. Whey protein isolate is also highly processed. Most whey protein isolates start from ultra-pasteurized conventional milk from animals raised on GMO feed, antibiotics, and other drugs. This milk is then exposed to acid processing, which strips out alkalizing minerals and naturally occurring vitamins and lipids. This processing makes whey protein isolate overly acidifying in the body. Chronically consuming whey protein isolate without the appropriate balance of alkalizing foods can acidify your body, which over time can increase your vulnerability to degenerative disease.

Another common plant-based protein source in protein powder is brown rice. Rice is often contaminated with arsenic, a highly toxic substance classified as carcinogenic to humans by the International Agency for Research on Cancer.[22] Arsenic is even found in organic brown rice, so you need to be very careful about the source and make sure the product has been tested for arsenic.

If a protein powder is not certified organic, the ingredients were likely treated with synthetic pesticides and may contain residues. Pesticides used on conventional farms are hormone disruptors, neurotoxins, or reproductive toxins that are strongly linked to many diseases and health issues. Roundup herbicide is commonly used on soy and it's also used as a desiccant (drying agent) on some nonorganic peas and flaxseed crops—all three of these are common ingredients in protein powder.

Almost every protein powder on the market contains natural flavors, which are practically the same thing as artificial flavors. Many brands contain artificial sweeteners such as sucralose or acesulfame potassium, which should be avoided if you want to protect your health. Besides, these types of sweeteners stimulate your appetite, increase sugar cravings, and promote fat storage and weight gain. Other brands are sweetened with stevia extract (instead of whole stevia leaf), which also goes through a chemical-laden process and can leave a bad aftertaste. This is why I prefer a protein powder that doesn't contain stevia.

Honestly, I couldn't find a protein powder on the market that met my high standards, so I created my own. Truvani plant-based vanilla protein has just five simple ingredients (and the chocolate flavor has only six), all of which are certified USDA Organic, non-GMO, and vegan. Each ingredient was hand-selected by me and the Truvani team. We tested each of them for heavy metals (such as lead), and they lived up to our standards. This holds true for one of the main ingredients, organic pea protein, which is often contaminated with lead. This is why we test ours at Truvani and went through multiple suppliers to find a clean source. If you are using another brand, be especially sure it has been tested for lead to avoid this harmful heavy metal in your protein drink!

Nut Butter: Avoid nut butters that contain added sugars and oils, as these are unnecessary. It's especially important to choose organic in this category because conventional peanuts and nuts are some of the most heavily sprayed crops. The best nut butters are raw, organic, and just one ingredient. Watch out for the "no stir" versions that contain added oils (usually palm oil) to keep them blended on the shelf. It's better to choose one that contains just one ingredient (nuts) and stir it yourself.

GRAINS

Bread: Many store-bought breads are made primarily with refined wheat flour, sugar, and unhealthy soybean oil. Refined grains are stripped of their nutrients and healthy fiber. Whole grains (grains that are not refined, such as whole wheat, which contains the entire grain—the bran, the germ, and the endosperm) have more fiber and other nutrients. The "multigrain" label simply means multiple types of grains are used in the product, but these may be refined grains.

If not organic, bread may potentially contain residues of synthetic pesticides. Wheat in particular is a grain that is sometimes treated pre-harvest with glyphosate (Roundup weed killer), and residues of this chemical have been found in some wheat products on the shelf. This practice is used only on conventional (nonorganic) wheat.

Although some organic wheat products have been contaminated with glyphosate, tests so far have found minimal glyphosate residue in them compared to nonorganic breads.[23]

Some breads, such as Ezekiel bread, are made with organic sprouted grains and absolutely no flour. This combination of sprouted grains contains all nine essential amino acids, which make up a complete protein. Because there are no preservatives in this brand, its products are found in the freezer section. Sprouted grains are more easily digested than starchy flour, and contain more vitamins, minerals, and antioxidants than whole grains. Phytic acid is destroyed when the grain sprouts, so your body is able to absorb the nutrients in these grains—which makes them that much better for you. Another brand, Organic Bread of Heaven, bakes traditional-style organic breads that are available online through mail order.

Pasta: Most store-bought pasta has likely been chemically bleached and completely stripped of its nutrients. It is then "enriched" with added vitamins from synthetic sources. Most wheat has been hybridized and damaged nutritionally during processing. The consumption of refined flour increases inflammation in the body and can disrupt the good intestinal bacteria in your digestive system.

As we've discussed, wheat is commonly contaminated with the herbicide Roundup, so it's important to always choose certified organic pasta to avoid ingredients that contain synthetic chemical residues. Ancient

BREAD

Poor choice:

* Wheat flour or other refined flours (not 100% whole grain)
* Not organic
* Soybean or canola oil
* Added sugars
* Dough conditioners (additives)

Misleading labels:

* "Wheat"
* "Multigrain"

Better choice:

* Sprouted grain
* Certified organic
* No added sugar
* No added oils

PASTA

Poor choice:

* Not organic
* Refined flour
* Synthetic vitamins

Better choice:

* Certified organic
* Made from lentils, 100% whole grains, or einkorn
* High in fiber and protein

RICE

Poor choice:

* Instant rice
* White rice
* Not organic

Better choice:

* Certified organic
* Tested for heavy metals
* Brown rice
* Brown basmati rice
* Wild rice
* Forbidden or black rice

CEREAL

Poor choice:

* Not organic
* Refined flour
* Artificial colors
* Caramel color
* Added flavors
* Added sugar and corn syrup
* Synthetic vitamins
* Preserved with BHT

Better choice:

* Certified organic
* Sprouted grains, nuts, seeds
* Low in added sugar
* Real food ingredients

CHICKEN or VEGETABLE BROTH

Poor choice:

* Not organic
* Added flavors
* MSG or hidden MSG additives

Better choice:

* Certified organic
* 100% real food ingredients
* Bone broth (the best are found in the freezer section)

grains are used to make some pastas, such as those in einkorn spaghetti. These are grains that haven't been hybridized over time and are more nutrient dense than the wheat that is produced today. Lentil pasta made from 100 percent lentils is a healthy alternative that is very high in protein and fiber, so it helps keep you feeling full longer.

Rice: White rice is a refined carbohydrate that has been stripped of its bran and germ, where the majority of nutrients reside. Refined carbohydrates such as white rice can spike blood sugar levels and tax your organs, slowing down healing and robbing the body of other important regulatory functions. Refined carbs can also cause weight gain that you can't seem to get rid of (especially around the midsection).

Brown rice is a whole grain—it is not refined and still contains its bran and germ (unlike white rice). Brown rice has a lower glycemic index than white rice and won't send your blood sugar surging. My personal preference is organic brown basmati rice, as it is not refined but still has a light and fluffy texture.

When choosing brands of rice it is a good idea to contact the companies that you buy rice from and ask them if they test for arsenic. Arsenic is a carcinogen that is prevalent in rice products, including some brands of brown rice (even organic). California-grown rice has been shown to contain lower amounts of arsenic than rice grown in other parts of the country, so consider where it is grown.

Cereal: Mainstream cereals are filled with cheap commodities such as corn and sugar, which are heavily refined, artificially flavored, and colored. They are so heavily processed that they do not have natural nutrients so most of them are sprayed with synthetic vitamins, minerals, and sometimes fortified with extra fiber and protein. It's the ultimate fake food. The preservative BHT, often seen in boxed cereals, is linked to cancer, and it's believed to be an endocrine disruptor that interferes with your hormones.[24]

While there are limited healthy cereal choices, you can select certified organic cereals that are minimally processed and made with real food: sprouted whole grains, oats, seeds, nuts, and dried fruit. Unfortunately, almost every packaged cold cereal contains added sugar. Look for those that are as low in sugar as possible, and sweetened with healthier alternatives such as maple syrup or honey. Keep in mind that just because a cereal is labeled non-GMO or organic does not mean it is made with nutritious ingredients. You still want to read those ingredient lists and watch that sugar content.

Chicken or Vegetable Broth: Just like any animal-based product, it is imperative to choose organic broth to avoid by-products from animals raised on GMO feed and synthetic drugs. Remember, the healthiest animals are raised on an organic pasture, not in a conventional factory farm. Some brands of broth contain strange ingredients that you wouldn't add to your bone broth at home, such as MSG, flavors, and even coconut milk. A high-quality broth requires no added

sweeteners, flavors, or additives. Instead, choose an organic brand that contains only 100 percent real food ingredients, just like you would use to make broth at home.

BEVERAGES

Nondairy Milk: Most popular nondairy milks (almond, coconut, oat, etc.) contain added sugar and flavors that are unnecessary. Eating too much sugar (which is easy to do, because it's in almost every processed food) leads to obesity, type 2 diabetes, heart disease, and even cancer. "Natural flavor" is practically the exact same thing as "artificial flavor," but it's derived from substances found in nature (plants, animals, etc.). Chemists create these complex formulations in a lab, isolating and blending specific flavors extracted from upward of hundreds of compounds.

Look for a certified organic milk to avoid ingredients treated with synthetic pesticides, but don't assume that all organic nut milks are healthy. Choose brands without added sugar, natural flavors, or carrageenan. Also try to find brands that don't include thickeners such as gellan gum, if possible.

Juice: Many bottled juices are made mostly from refined sugar and water, followed by juice concentrates. You can find this by reading the ingredient list. To make a concentrate, fruit is heated into a syrup and then water is added back in, which destroys nutrients. The concentration process involves both adding and subtracting chemicals and natural plant by-products in order to condense the juice.

JUICE

Poor choice:

* Mostly sugar and water
* Made with concentrates
* Added flavors
* Not organic

Better choice:

* Raw
* Cold-pressed
* Organic
* No added sugar
* No added flavors
* No juice concentrates

NONDAIRY MILK

Poor choice:

* Not organic
* Added sugar
* Added flavor
* Unnecessary "gums"
* Carrageenan

Better choice:

* Certified organic
* No added sugar
* No added flavor
* No added thickeners
* Real food ingredients

BOTTLED WATER

Poor choice

* Purified tap water
* Plastic bottle

Better choice:

* Home filtered water
* Mountain spring water
* Glass or stainless steel bottle

TEA

Poor choice:

* Not organic
* Added flavors
* Added sweeteners
* Harmful packaging

Better choice:

* Certified organic
* 100% tea, herbs, and spices
* No added flavors
* No added sweeteners
* Safe packaging or loose leaf

Don't fall for juice labels like "100% Vitamin C" and "100% Juice" to choose the best option. Food companies are allowed to say "100% juice" on the label even though their juice contains additives, flavorings, or preservatives. Also, the "100% Vitamin C" label may be there because synthetic vitamin C has been added to juice concentrates, sugar, and water, while trying to fool you into believing the vitamin C inside is from nutritious fruit used to make the juice. Always check the ingredient label.

It is absolutely critical that you choose organic juice first and foremost to avoid synthetic pesticides. In an ideal world, you would always be able to consume a raw cold-pressed juice straight out of a juicer so its enzymes, vitamins, and minerals are still intact. The next best thing is juice that is preserved with high-pressure processing (HPP). This method retains food quality, maintains freshness, and extends microbiological shelf life without the addition of heat. A high level of cool pressure is applied evenly to destroy any pathogens and ensure the juice is safe to drink while preserving nutrients.

Water: Popular brands like Aquafina (by PepsiCo) and Dasani (by Coca-Cola) are just purified tap water.[25] They take their water from city water systems, run it through more filtering, bottle it, and sell it at a huge markup. Look for the terms *public water*, *municipal source*, or *community water* on bottles; this indicates it's filtered tap water. But brands aren't required to disclose this. Bottles that say "artesian" or "spring" water typically are not from the tap, but are more expensive and usually still packaged in plastic that is horrible for our environment and may leach chemicals into the water.

It simply doesn't make much sense to buy filtered tap water when you can do the same for yourself at home. If you want to save yourself a ton of money and protect our environment, stop buying bottled water altogether (unless you're traveling or have a specific need, of course). There is a time and a place for bottled water, but getting a good water filtering system for your home is the way to go in the long run. You can invest in a stainless steel water bottle and fill it up before you head out. When you're away from home for an extended time, are traveling, or do not have access to water at your home due to an emergency or other circumstances, choose mountain spring water in glass bottles whenever possible.

Tea: Most tea is not washed before it is put into bags, which means if the tea was sprayed with pesticides, those pesticides go directly into your cup. Many brands of nonorganic tea have been tested and shown to have high pesticide levels.[26] Imagine what happens when pesticide-laden tea is steeped in boiling water. This is why it is important to choose organic tea, which is regulated to prohibit the use of synthetic pesticides, many of which are known carcinogens and developmental toxins.

Another popular ingredient in tea is "natural flavors," used to trick consumers into thinking they are buying better, cleaner ingredients; however, companies are just covering up the inferior taste and low quality of their tea.

Although the actual tea bag is not an ingredient like the tea and herbs inside, it is an element that is put into boiling water, so you want to consider what it is made out of and whether it can leach harmful chemicals into your drink. Tea bags are most commonly made from food-grade nylon or polyethylene terephthalate (PET), which may potentially break down when steeped in boiling water. While the plastic won't melt in your tea, the glass transition temperature could leak out harmful phthalates.[27] Beware that some of the newer "silky" tea bags are made with a variety of plastics. Some plastics are nylon, some are made of viscose rayon, and others are made of thermoplastic, PVC, or polypropylene. Another thing to watch out for are paper tea bags, as they may be treated with epichlorohydrin, a potential carcinogen.

Choose a certified organic brand of tea and check the ingredient list on the package to see if there are any added flavors or other ingredients such as sweeteners. Make sure the brand you buy uses a safe form of packaging material, or buy loose-leaf tea and use a stainless steel or glass tea strainer. Have the company verify that its bags do not contain epichlorohydrin, and avoid plastic tea bags altogether. This information will likely not be on the label, so it takes a bit of research (you may need to call the company to ask). Personally I love Rishi Tea and Numi Organic Tea.

SNACKS AND TREATS

Chips and Crackers: Packaged snacks such as chips and crackers can be land mines. Even ones that appear healthy are often full of GMOs, sugar, MSG, and processed additives. A common ingredient, GMO corn, is not a healthy grain and is likely contaminated with Roundup weed killer. Snacks made with flours (wheat, white rice, etc.) are not a healthy choice either because flour is a heavily refined product, and is considered a "dead" food with no real nutritional value.

Look for organic snacks composed of 100 percent whole grains and seeds without added sugar or additives, such as Flackers or Mary's Gone Crackers. It's a good idea to limit intake of processed snacks in general, and instead choose fresh veggie sticks, fruits, nuts, or seeds.

Bars: Even the bars considered the "cleanest" out there often are not. Snack and protein bars are usually heavily processed and hardly resemble real food. Avoid bars that are not organic and that are made with added sugar, artificial sweeteners (including sucralose or acesulfame potassium), "natural flavors," artificial colors, heavily processed proteins, and other additives that are not real food. Instead, look for organic bars composed of real food (nuts, seeds, fruit) and free of so-called natural flavors. To choose a clean bar, ask yourself, "Would I find these ingredients in my Food Babe Kitchen?"

Fruit Snacks: Most packaged fruit snacks are not a good option, even when they say "Made with Real Fruit" on the packaging. They are essentially candy, made with heat-treated fruit purees and concentrated juices, corn syrup, sugar, fake flavors, and artificial dyes. The main ingredient in many fruit snacks is processed apple "concentrate" or "puree." Apple concentrate is not the same as whole apples. To make a concentrate, fruit puree or juice is heated into a syrup, which makes it higher in sugar,

CHIPS and CRACKERS

Poor choice:

* Not organic
* GMO corn
* Sunflower, canola, or soybean oil
* Added sugar
* Added flavors
* MSG and hidden MSG
* Artificial colors
* Rice flour (not whole grain)

Better choice:

* Certified organic
* 100% whole grains and seeds
* No added sugar
* Real spices instead of "flavors"
* No yeast extract or hydrolyzed protein (hidden MSG)

BARS

Poor choice:

* Not organic
* Added flavors
* Added sugar
* Artificial sweeteners
* Artificial colors
* Heavily processed proteins (such as soy isolate)

Better choice:

* Certified organic
* Real food ingredients
* No added flavors
* No refined sugar

FRUIT SNACKS

Poor choice:

* Fruit concentrates
* Fruit purees
* Artificial colors
* Added flavors
* Added sugar and sweeteners
* Added synthetic vitamins
* Not organic

Better choice:

* Certified organic
* Dried fruit
* Freeze-dried fruit
* Fresh whole fruit
* Only one ingredient (fruit)

CHOCOLATE and CANDY

Poor choice:

* Not organic
* Artificial colors
* Added flavors
* Vanillin
* Preservatives (such as TBHQ or BHT)
* Corn syrup or high-fructose corn syrup

Better choice:

* Certified organic
* No artificial colors or flavors
* No preservatives

ICE CREAM

Poor choice:

* Not organic
* Artificial colors
* Artificial flavors
* Artificial sweeteners
* Cellulose gum
* Polysorbate 80
* Monoglycerides and diglycerides
* Carrageenan

Better choice:

* Certified organic
* No emulsifiers
* No added flavors or colors
* 100% real food ingredients

lower in fiber, and lower in nutrients than whole fruit.

Oftentimes, the flavor of the fruit snack does not actually include that specific fruit (e.g., a strawberry snack without any strawberries). Companies artificially flavor and dye the apple concentrate to taste and look like strawberries or other fruits, because it's cheaper to produce. People assume they're eating strawberries but they are actually eating artificial colors and flavors. Even organic versions of fruit snacks are heavily processed, full of sugar, and hardly have any nutrient value.

Instead of "fruit snacks," try dried or freeze-dried fruit instead. Look for brands that are organic and have only one ingredient: fruit. Better yet, choose and enjoy fresh whole fruit.

Chocolate and Candy: Of course, all candy is going to contain sugar and is not considered a health food, but I am including this category here because almost everyone purchases candy for the holidays and also enjoys it from time to time. While candy consumption should be limited overall, if you are going to indulge, make sure you are doing it the right way!

Popular mainstream candy brands use corn syrup, artificial colors, and artificial flavors almost exclusively to make their products. A common artificial flavor used in candy is vanillin, which is made from wood or petrochemicals. Seek out more natural brands that do not use these substances. Also watch out for such preservatives as BHT or TBHQ in your candy. BHT is banned and heavily restricted in other countries because it is linked to cancer, and TBHQ is linked to asthma, allergies, and dermatitis.[28] As with anything else, choose organic candy whenever possible to reduce exposure to harmful pesticides. This is especially important for chocolate, which may be laced with pesticides from conventional farming practices.

Ice Cream: First and foremost, because it is an animal product, it is imperative to choose organic ice cream. Almost all nonorganic dairy cows in the United States are fed a diet of genetically modified (GMO) grains on a factory farm. When cows eat GMOs, they are eating Roundup herbicide too. The primary ingredient in Roundup—glyphosate—is linked to cancer. Testing has found other pesticides, antibiotics, and drugs in conventional nonorganic milk (including ones that are banned), and this is what you could be consuming when you eat nonorganic ice cream. Organically raised cows are permitted to eat only organic non-GMO food and organic grass. Ultimately, you want to look for certified organic ice cream to avoid dairy raised with herbicide-laden GMOs, hormones, antibiotics, and all the drugs that are prohibited on organic farms.

Thankfully, when you choose organic ice cream you avoid artificial flavors or artificial colors because neither are permitted in organic products. However, some organic brands contain unhealthy emulsifiers, including carrageenan or cellulose gum, and "natural flavors" that as we've discussed are essentially the same as artificial flavors. Look for brands that don't take these shortcuts and that are flavored naturally with vanilla beans, lemon, cinnamon, cocoa, and the like, and that are made entirely with real food ingredients.

The Food Babe Kitchen Pantry List

I have put together a list of all my pantry staples, including brand names that I love and everything that I stock in my fridge and freezer—you can download a printable version of it from FoodBabe.com/resources.

I highly recommend using my list as a guide and then creating a list of your own, adding your favorite brands and things that you like to stock in your own pantry. Keep a copy of this list handy, pehaps on your fridge or inside your pantry door. Simply check off anything that needs to be replaced each week; this will make it easy for you to build your grocery shopping list. Keep this list handy on your computer for extra copies, or get fancy and laminate it to use with a dry erase marker and just circle what you need to buy each week.

CREATING A SAFE AND NONTOXIC KITCHEN

Since having children, whenever we travel we always look for a rental that allows us to have access to a full kitchen—but there is always one big problem. When we arrive, we find the kitchen stocked with horrible cleaning products. You know, like that bright blue dish soap? This is why I bring my own. The cupboards also always hold cheap Teflon pans, which is why I often travel with a nontoxic cooking pan in my luggage too. This got me thinking. There is still so much educating to do about the hazardous chemicals in certain cleaning products and specific types of cookware. After I learned about these hazards years ago, I stocked my kitchen with nontoxic accessories and cleaners, and I believe that everyone should have a Food Babe Kitchen. It's much easier to create than you may think. Here's how to get started:

Pots and Pans

It is very important to consider the pots and pans you cook with because toxic chemicals have been used in the production of some cookware, and some types of cookware can gas off harmful chemicals into the air. The company DuPont used the chemical perfluorooctanoic acid (PFOA) for decades in the manufacture of Teflon,[29] that popular coating of nonstick cookware. It's been shown that Teflon releases a toxic gas when heated that can make people sick. Although the FDA has since issued a ban of PFCs (compounds used to make nonstick pans), many older pans could contain these banned substances. And although now all newly made Teflon-coated pans are PFOA-free, they can still release potentially harmful substances into the air when heavily heated, leading to a condition called polymer fume fever, aka "Teflon flu."[30] Yikes. Avoid the risks of Teflon and nonstick cookware by choosing these instead:

- Stainless steel cookware and baking pans, which are relatively inexpensive and last a long time. Stainless steel bowls are great as well.

- Cast-iron pans that are properly seasoned make great substitutes for nonstick coated pans and are perfect for high-heat cooking. They also last forever if cared for properly.

- Glass baking pans are perfect for breads and casseroles.

- Other safe options include ceramic or stoneware pans.

Food Storage

Food storage containers made from plastics contain endocrine-disrupting chemicals, such as BPA, which can migrate into the food stored in them, especially if the food is ever hot in them. Even "BPA-free" plastic containers can harbor toxins and estrogen disruptors,[31] and you don't want that touching your food. These endocrine-disrupting chemicals mess with the hormones in your body, which can lead to cancer and other diseases. Glass and stainless steel are much safer, and there are many, many options available everywhere.

Do yourself a favor and invest in a set of oven-safe glass and stainless steel food storage containers. Not only do they last much longer than plastic containers (no staining!), they won't leach dangerous chemicals into your food. I like to use inexpensive glass jars to store homemade soups, stews, smoothies, dressings, chia pudding, nuts, juices . . . the list goes on. They come in a variety of sizes, so it's easy to pack jars in individual portions. When bringing food to the office or away from home, stainless steel containers are ideal because they are lighter than glass and there's zero risk of breaking (although I haven't had any problems with glass containers breaking; they are very sturdy, but heavy). Pantry items such as flour, oats, and coffee can also be stored in glass containers, which come in a variety of sizes. When freezing homemade leftovers, I like to put them in silicone trays that have individual portions. That way I can just pop out one portion to defrost and reheat at a time—this is perfect for parents with young children!

It's estimated that about two million plastic bags are used every minute worldwide.[32] Two million every minute! Isn't that insane? Most of these bags are just used once and thrown in the trash. This is all contributing to massive landfills and polluting our environment. Each and every one of us can reduce this mountain of trash by packing our food with reusable and nontoxic products. Look for reusable sandwich bags made from nontoxic materials; these clean easily in the dishwasher too. As far as plastic wrap goes, I limit the amount I use as much as possible and make sure that it doesn't touch the food that I'm covering. Sometimes I'll just cover a dish of food with a plate instead.

Slow Cooker

This is a must-have appliance in any kitchen. A slow cooker makes it so easy to prepare an entire meal to feed a crowd with very little hands-on time, and it will be all ready to eat whenever you are. Some of my favorite recipes to make in a slow cooker include beans and oats. I personally use a small slow cooker almost every evening to cook steel-cut oats overnight (recipe on page 71), so they're ready to eat in the morning. This is the easiest inexpensive breakfast!

Not all slow cookers are safe, however. The coating in some slow cookers contains lead, a potent neurotoxin, which can leach into every slow-cooked meal you make. Certain foods, such as those that are acidic, are at a greater risk along with the time and temperature in which those foods are cooked. When purchasing a slow cooker, make sure that the manufacturer has tested the coating for lead and has concluded that the glaze on the bowl does not include or leach lead into your food while cooking. This information is readily found by calling the manufacturer or checking its website (if not disclosed, likely lead testing isn't being done).

Towels and Napkins

Almost every kitchen has a roll of paper towels in it, but you may want to rethink whether you want one in yours. Most paper towels are made from wood and then treated with chlorine to whiten them. This is an issue because the bleaching forms dioxins, which are terrible chemicals linked to cancer. Dioxins are leached into the air and water supply, harming not just you but also plants, animals, and your environment. This is why I do my best to use the least amount of paper towels as possible in my house. When I do use paper towels, I buy unbleached and recycled versions. I greatly prefer to use organic cotton towels and napkins that I simply wash and reuse. We use these in my kitchen just like you'd use a disposable paper towel: for everyday cleaning, cleaning up spills, and as napkins at the table. They are much more absorbent, and look nice too. Sure, there is a minor expense up front to purchase your reusable towels, but you'll save so much money down the road as you won't be buying big packages of paper towels anymore.

Cleaning Products

Washing your dishes with potentially toxic chemicals makes no sense. The chemicals get on your hands, where they get a free pass through your skin and into your bloodstream. As with all the cleaning products in my house, I keep dish soaps and dishwasher detergents simple in composition and search out nontoxic formulas. Some nasty ingredients that you want to avoid in your cleaning products include:

- Triclosan
- Chloroxylenol
- Methylisothiazolinone
- Phosphates
- Synthetic dyes (stick with clear cleaning products)
- Fragrances

For cleaning countertops, basic essentials such as baking soda and vinegar are inexpensive and work great! Whatever you do, steer clear of the antibacterial cleansers and wipes. It's been shown that these are not more effective than simply using soap and water and may contribute to antibiotic-resistant bacteria.

Kitchen Swaps

In some cases, the tools you cook with can be just as important as the ingredients you are cooking! Here are some easy swaps that you can make in your own kitchen to reduce your reliance on household goods that are unhealthy for our bodies and the environment. Don't feel the need to make all of these swaps overnight. Start with the items that you use most often in your household to make the most impact. Consider gifting safe kitchen items to your loved ones to help them create non-toxic kitchens as well. There is a printable version of this list at FoodBabe.com/resources to share with friends and family.

INSTEAD OF THIS	USE THIS
Non-stick Teflon coated pots and pans	Cast iron, stainless steel, and ceramic pots and pans
Cooking spray	Organic coconut oil, butter, avocado, or olive oil (no spray) and unbleached parchment paper for baking
Plastic storage containers (even BPA-Free)	Glass, stainless steel, or silicone storage containers
Plastic bags	Reusable non-toxic silicone bags
Plastic wrap	Reusable beeswax wraps, silicone toppers, plates or glass containers with lids
Antibacterial, dyed, and scented dish soap	Natural non-toxic dish soap (fragrance-free and dye-free)
Bleached paper napkins	Washable organic cotton napkins
Bleached paper towels	Recycled unbleached paper towels or washable organic cotton towels
Aluminum foil	Unbleached parchment paper or a reusable Silpat silicone mat
Microwave	Countertop toaster oven
Tap water and plastic bottled water	Water filter and glass bottled water
Plastic utensils	Wood and stainless steel utensils
Baking powder	Aluminum-free baking powder
Aluminum baking pans	Glass, stainless steel and ceramic bakeware
Antibacterial, dyed, scented cleaning products and bleach	Natural, non-toxic cleaning products (fragrance-free and dye-free) and/or vinegar and baking soda
Ionized salt	Sea salt and Himalayan salt
Bleached and dyed baking cups	Silicone or unbleached parchment baking cups
Plastic water kettle	Stainless steel or glass water kettle
Plastic straws	Glass or stainless steel straws
Plastic and melamine dishes for kids	Bamboo dishes and silicone baking cups

Cooking Spray
(you don't need it!)

Cooking spray is technically a food item, but it is a staple in most kitchens and worth mentioning here. I don't use cooking spray. Although I get how it is convenient to spray a dish, it is really unnecessary. Almost all cooking sprays out there, even organic ones, are made with inferior oils such as canola oil and corn oil along with preservatives, emulsifiers, and compressed gases derived from petroleum to help the oil spray from the can. I prefer not to use products with unnecessary, heavily processed, and potentially harmful ingredients whenever possible. You can simply dab a thin layer of organic coconut oil, butter, avocado, or olive oil into your pan—no spray needed. When baking cookies or using a baking sheet, I line it with unbleached parchment paper or a reusable Silpat silicone mat.

Reheating Food

What I'm about to say is somewhat controversial. I never use a microwave. Never. I have one because it came with my house, but I don't use it to reheat food nor can I remember the last time I used one anywhere. That doesn't mean that everything I eat is freshly cooked—actually far from it. I'm a big fan of preparing food ahead of time, eating leftovers, and utilizing my freezer to keep homemade food handy, especially for my daughter. I simply heat up soups and chili on the stovetop. I'll use my regular oven for reheating large portions of food, but often use a large toaster oven, which uses less power and heats up a plate of leftovers in about eight minutes.

I simply place my food on oven-safe plates to reheat in my oven or toaster oven. When the food is heated up, I remove it with an oven mitt on and place it on a heat-resistant place mat or trivet. Of course, if I'm giving the food to my daughter, I will remove the food from the hot plate and place it on a different plate for her, so she doesn't burn herself. It couldn't be easier and there really is no need for a microwave in our life.

Filtered water

It is vitally important that you drink and cook with clean filtered water. Water straight from your tap that isn't properly filtered may be tainted with contaminants, such as:

- Pesticides
- Fluoride
- Bacteria and viruses
- Aluminum
- Chromium 6
- Radioactive materials
- Arsenic
- Prescription drugs
- Chlorine
- Parasites
- Disinfection byproducts
- Lead

These substances may cause health issues after long-term exposure, which is why filtered water is crucial to your health. Instead of buying bottled water for everyday use, investing in a good water filtration system in your home is a better option. That's because bottled water is often very expensive, packaged in plastic, and in some cases, simply glorified tap water. Many popular bottled water brands take their water from city water systems, run it through more filtering, bottle it, and sell it at a huge markup. Bottles labeled as "artesian" or "spring" water are not from the tap, but are still expensive and usually packaged in plastic that is horrible for our environment. You can save thousands of dollars in the long run if you filter your own water at home.

Good water filtration systems are certified to remove and reduce chlorine, chloramines, heavy metals, chlorine-resistant cysts, herbicides, pesticides, VOCs, and pharmaceuticals. If you'd like to filter out fluoride, look for a reverse osmosis system that is certified to filter all the above contaminants and fluoride.

If you're on a tight budget start out with a countertop or faucet water filter, which also works well if you are renting your home. A step-up would be an under-the-counter model, which installs easily under your sink. For the most complete solution, you can invest in a whole house filter. This gives you the peace of mind that the water from every tap in your home is filtered, including your shower. I personally love knowing that I can get clean water from every tap in the house.

WHY EVERYONE SHOULD HAVE A FOOD BABE KITCHEN

By making these changes to your kitchen, you will:

- Reduce waste by eliminating the use of disposable and plastic food packaging that clogs up our landfills and oceans;

- Save money by reducing the use of expensive single-use packaging and disposable products;

- Eat healthier food by making it easier to store homemade foods, reducing your reliance on packaged processed food;

- Protect your health by using nontoxic containers and supplies that don't leach risky chemicals into your food; and

- Promote sustainability by supporting brands that are doing the right things in creating nontoxic products that are good for our bodies and the planet.

Everyone should have a Food Babe Kitchen. Don't you agree?

chapter 2
BECOME A FOOD BABE

Right after a health crisis in my early 20s, the first thing I wanted to do was lose weight and look better. At first, I believed what everyone else around me was saying and looked to everyone else for answers. I respected authority figures and companies and followed them blindly, as many people do today.

Organizations such as Weight Watchers told me I could eat virtually anything I wanted as long as I checked the calories or points, carbs, and fat grams. Although I followed their plan, I always found myself struggling to maintain my weight. Their advice left me with no energy and feeling hungry all the time.

I outsourced my meals to restaurants such as Subway who told me their food would help me "Eat Fresh" and that I'd lose weight like Jared did if I ate their sandwiches. I believed them and so many other restaurant chains that were serving me industrial chemicals instead of real food.

Everything I believed for most of my life was turned upside down as I investigated and looked deeper into what I was really eating. One day it all clicked! My biggest lesson learned was that I cannot outsource my health or my food.

I could not continue letting the food industry dictate for me what was healthy. I could not continue trusting "diet programs," and I most definitely could not trust marketing from food companies and restaurants to help me make my food decisions. As a result, I started to learn how to cook and prepare my own food at home as much as possible.

Most of us have become accustomed to obtaining the majority of our meals from restaurants and the processed-food industry, but all too often this leads to obesity and disease—and making us feel downright awful on a routine basis. Getting yourself in your kitchen each day to making homemade meals can be daunting at first, but I've come to find that half the battle is meal planning.

WHY YOU SHOULD
PLAN YOUR MEALS

Always thinking about what to eat next can be stressful, and figuring out something healthy to cook at the last minute totally sucks. If you like to wing it and don't plan out your meals each week, beware that life can get in the way and throw your plan for healthy eating totally off track. Next thing you know, you'll be ordering pizza and wings on speed dial. It seems all too easy to just pick up some takeout in the evening and relax on the couch, but I've learned that even when I'm crunched for time, I can't continuously eat out at restaurants if I want to maintain an ideal weight and stay in the best health that I've ever known.

When you cook your own meals you are in control of the ingredients and know everything that goes into them. It's the only way to know exactly what you are eating. Meal planning and cooking at home with whole real foods is an optimal way to stay alkaline, provide your body an abundant amount of nutrients on a daily basis, and prevent disease. That's why I prepare at least 15 home-cooked meals every week. That's at least five homemade breakfasts, five homemade lunches, and five homemade dinners each week—and usually more.

Having a meal plan has been absolutely crucial to my success; I'd never be able to do it otherwise. Meal planning makes it so much easier to know what to buy and cook each month without getting bored of the same old dishes. Planning out your meals makes living in this crazy food world actually simple.

Planning out your meals can also save you a ton of money. If you find yourself making last-minute shopping trips several times a week to pick up items you're missing for dinner (or calling in for takeout), you are probably spending more money than you need to—and probably wasting more food too. When you plan meals, it's easier to use the same bulk ingredients in multiple recipes and to take advantage of sales. You can even write your plan to include items that are advertised as being on sale, which is virtually impossible to do when you are running to the store in a rush to get dinner on the table. It's really nice knowing that your meals for the week are planned out and that your kitchen is stocked with everything you'll need. Do this every week and it will save your life.

GETTING STARTED
WITH MEAL PLANNING

If you're new to getting on the meal-planning bandwagon, I encourage you to start small. Plan on bringing specific lunches to work every day for a week. Or perhaps it's just breakfast that you plan at first. Start by planning one meal a day and then gradually increase to 15 planned meals a week, or whichever goal seems comfortable to you. Everyone likes to plan their meals differently, but I can't emphasize enough how important it is to *have a plan*.

There are essentially two phases to meal planning:

1. Deciding what meals you want to make

2. Shopping for the meals you want to make

The first step can be pretty easy. You simply take out a sheet of paper, write out the days of the week, thumb through this cookbook, and plug in recipes for each day. You can also search for recipes that you have collected online or sift through handwritten recipes that you've kept. If the recipe is from a cookbook, make sure to note the cookbook name and page number in your meal plan so that it's easy for you to find when it's time to cook.

This manual method of creating a meal plan works well for a lot of people, but there are other ways to do it. The most important thing is to create a system for yourself to make it as easy as possible. There are apps available that you can download to your phone or computer. You can also use a calendar that you either hang on your wall or log into on your computer. I've created a printable calendar specially designed for healthy meal planning that you can download (find it at FoodBabe.com/resources). Each week, just fill one out, print it, and hang it up somewhere in your kitchen.

After you've got your plan written out for the week, it's time to shop! Pick a convenient day to do your shopping. Try to purchase everything you will need for an entire week during one trip, as this will save you a lot of time. This also ensures that when it comes time to cook a meal, you'll have everything you need and avoid those last-minute trips to the store.

It is vitally important that you bring a shopping list with you to the store—and stick to it. This helps you remember everything you need and avoid impulse buys. Researchers at the University of Pennsylvania found that consumers who avoid impulse shopping can shave roughly 20 percent off their grocery bills![1] Grocery stores know this and play on your weaknesses with displays at the end of each aisle and in the checkout line, enticing you to add more items to your cart—usually junk food. This is also why grocery stores are designed in a way that makes it harder for you to find everything you need in one section of the store. They want you to walk down each aisle, to increase the possibility that you will feel compelled to buy more, and more, and more. One way to avoid this is to do your grocery shopping online, an option now offered by many major grocery stores for either pickup or delivery (for a small fee). When placing your order online, make sure to stick to your shopping list and simply add what you need. You'll likely find that the fee for this service pays for itself in the time and money you save!

So how do you create a shopping list? Some apps and websites will automatically create shopping lists for you based on your meal plan. However, you can easily do this with no special equipment. One way to make writing a shopping list easy is to keep a healthy pantry list. This is a list of everything that you try to keep on hand in your pantry (download mine from FoodBabe .com/resources). Print several copies of your pantry list and use a new one each week. With your recipes nearby, check off each item that you already have in your kitchen, then add anything that is not checked off to your shopping list. Include the fresh produce and meats to your shopping list that you will need to round out each meal. You may find some recipes include rare items that are not on your pantry list; for instance, a curry may call for turmeric, not something you normally keep on hand or on your pantry list. Just write this down on your shopping list. Finally, add any healthy perishable snacks, such as some apples, celery, or carrots that you'd like to have on hand for grab-and-go.

Finally, take a few minutes to review the websites of your favorite grocery stores to see if they have any promotions or coupons available. Use this opportunity to add extra items to your list to take advantage of sale prices on pantry items that you use often. Are they offering 25 percent off organic spices? Now may be a great time to stock up the spice rack.

You will find that over time this method is a money saver. You'll acquire a fuller pantry each week, and will not need to buy as much to make your meals. A few key healthy pantry items will be used in several meals, such as vegetable (or chicken) broth, pureed tomatoes, beans, rice, quinoa, spices, and oats. Once you have these on hand at all times, healthy eating will become easier and less expensive!

HOW TO PLAN YOUR MEALS LIKE A FOOD BABE

- Take a quick tour of your fridge, freezer, and pantry. Write down the perishable ingredients you already have that you can use for meals next week. Do you have a head of broccoli, almond butter, and brown rice noodles? Perhaps you can plan to make Pad Thai (recipe on page 177) without needing to buy more ingredients. This not only saves money, but prevents food waste!

- Store your recipes in a handy space. Keep a handful of healthy cookbooks (including this one) on a special shelf to help you create your meal plans. I like to bookmark my favorite recipes. Recipes from the Internet can be saved to Pinterest, Facebook, or other online apps designed for saving recipes. You can also print them out to put them in a binder, organized by category. This way you create your own personalized cookbook!

- Write your shopping list at the same time you schedule your recipes. With your recipes in front of you, you can make sure your shopping list is detailed with everything you need in one trip.

- Keep your go-to favorite recipes on repeat. If you find that fish tacos (recipe on page 178) are quick and easy to make on a weeknight and that the whole family cleans their plates, make a note to repeat it each week, or every other week. Try picking just one lunch or breakfast and make it for a few days in a row. You don't need variety in all meals every single day. When you make a new recipe that everyone loves, don't forget to add it to the weekly rotation!

- Search for fun new recipes to try. This will give you some inspiration to get in the kitchen and try something new. Flip through cookbooks and check out foodie websites for ideas. Consider using ingredients that you've never used before. Try to prepare at least one new recipe each week to keep cooking interesting for you and to bring variety to your table.

- Don't try to plan everything. No one is perfect. You'll find that even when you have a carefully crafted plan in place, you won't always stick to it. As a goal, try to write out your plan with no more than five

dinners each week. Leave room in your schedule for nights when you just eat leftovers or everyone fends for themselves with what you have on hand. It's inevitable that there will be a few days when you won't feel like cooking, so take the pressure off yourself!

- Stick to the seasons. It's less expensive and healthier to plan your meals with seasonal ingredients. Seasonal produce tends to be grown locally and harvested at its peak freshness. Consider signing up for local produce delivery services or a CSA (community supported agriculture) subscription, which automates seasonal eating while supporting local farmers.

- Keep holidays, special events, and the weather in mind. The kids have a basketball game after school on Tuesday? Plan to make something quick and easy that night or use a meal that you have stored in the freezer. If there is snow in the forecast on Thursday, that would be a great night to plan on a hearty soup or stew. If you know you're heading out of town on Friday and won't be eating at home for a few days, plan for Thursday meals that will use up perishable ingredients and leftovers you've already got in the fridge.

- Be flexible. Inevitably, there will come a time when you are not in the mood for tacos on your planned "taco night." Feel free to swap that meal with another recipe that you had planned later in the week. You should always cook what sounds good at the time, without straying too much from your plan whenever possible.

- Use the same ingredients in multiple recipes. If you buy a whole chicken, use it to make two meals with shredded chicken (and make homemade broth too!). Buy a large head of cauliflower to make roasted veggies one night and then toss the leftovers into soup the next night. Finding ways to use your leftovers is a big money saver.

- Have weekly theme nights. Pick different types of meals that your family loves and assign each one a day. For instance, Sunday can be soup night, Tuesday can be taco night, and Thursday can be veggie stir-fry night. Then all you need to do is pick which soup (or taco, or stir-fry) recipe you want to include in your meal plan each week.

- Get your family involved. Ask them what their favorite meals are or ask them to flip through this cookbook and pick out what they like. Do this with the little ones in your household too! They may surprise you and add some fun and unique meals that you'd never choose on your own.

Don't Like an Ingredient? No Problem.

You're ready to begin cooking dinner and suddenly notice you are missing an ingredient . . . oh, no! Or perhaps you (or someone in your family) has food allergies to specific ingredients or simply doesn't like them, and you're having a hard time finding the right recipes to make. That's where this Ingredient Substitution Guide comes in handy. Next time you find yourself unable to use an ingredient in a recipe, check this list to quickly swap it out for something else. Most of the recipes found in the *Food Babe Kitchen* are flexible and easily customizable to meet your preferences.

INGREDIENT SUBSTITUTION GUIDE

VEGETABLES

Eggplant	Mushrooms	Brussels sprouts	Onions	Peppers
Zucchini	Eggplant	Cauliflower	Garlic	Celery
Yellow squash	Zucchini	Broccoli	Leeks	Cucumbers
Mushrooms	Cauliflower	Artichokes	Shallots	Tomatoes

Beets	Kale	Artichokes	Broccoli	Spinach
Carrots	Arugula	Asparagus	Cauliflower	Kale
Sweet potato	Spinach	Kohlrabi hearts	Green cabbage	Romaine
Red cabbage	Swiss chard	Heart of palm	Broccoli rabe	Swiss chard

Bok choy	Cucumber	Butternut squash	Carrots	Celery
Beet greens	Celery	Sweet potato	Sweet potato	Zucchini
Kale	Zucchini	Carrots	Squash	Cucumber
Dandelion greens	Jicama	Spaghetti squash	Parsnips	Jicama

FRUIT

Avocado	Banana	Tomato	Apple	Lime
Chayote squash	Avocado	Red pepper	Pear	Lemon
Artichoke	Mango	Radish	Grapes	Orange
Banana	Papaya	Beets	Peach	Tangerine

GRAINS AND BEANS

Quinoa	Oats	Beans	Wheat flour	Tortillas
Brown rice	Quinoa	Mushrooms	Buckwheat flour	Collard leaves
Bulgar	Barley	Sweet potato	Oat flour	Cabbage
Cauliflower	Buckwheat groats	Cauliflower	Almond flour	Coconut wraps

HERBS AND SPICES

Cilantro	Parsley	Mint	Curry powder	Ginger
Parsley	Cilantro	Basil	Ginger	Lemon
Basil	Arugula	Ginger	Coriander	Fennel
Chives	Kale	Parsley	Fenugreek	Garlic

LEAN PROTEINS

Beef	Chicken	Turkey	Fish	Eggs (in baking)
Chicken	Lamb	Lamb	Chicken	Banana
Tofu/tempeh	Tofu/tempeh	Tofu/tempeh	Tofu/tempeh	Ground flaxseed
Beans	Beans	Beans	Beans	Applesauce
Mushrooms	Mushrooms	Mushrooms	Mushrooms	

DAIRY AND NONDAIRY

Goat cheese	Yogurt	Nut milk	Butter	Coconut milk
Feta	Sour cream	Oat milk	Coconut butter	Nut milk
Nutritional yeast	Coconut milk	Hemp milk	Coconut oil	Yogurt
Crumbled tofu	Almond yogurt	Cow's milk	Olive oil	Rice milk

PANTRY

Coconut oil	Nuts/nut butter	Vinegar	Honey	Coconut
Olive oil	Sunflower seeds	Apple cider vinegar	Maple syrup	Chopped nuts
Avocado oil	Pumpkin seeds	Red wine vinegar	Coconut palm nectar	Sliced almonds
Sesame oil	Sesame seeds	Lemon		Rolled oats

SAVE TIME WITH MEAL PREPPING

Some people like to add an additional step to their meal planning by doing some, if not all, meal prepping at the start of the week. This is when you prepare entire meals, meal components, and snacks, or prewash and cut up produce that you plan to eat during the week so it's ready to go. This is optional, of course, but will make busy mornings, work-time lunches, and lazy weeknights much easier.

If you'd like to delve into meal prepping, start slowly. Take a look at all the recipes in your meal plan and determine which items are the most time-consuming or messy to prepare (often these are beans, rice, nut milk, and meat); focus on prepping only a few of those items when you have time. Prep the meals that will save you the most hassle during the week, according to your lifestyle. For instance, if you have really busy mornings, it makes sense to prep your breakfasts ahead of time. Likewise, if you're always running around at night, prep as many dinner items as possible so that meal is easier to get on the table.

Prepping homemade sauces, seasoning mixes, and dressings ahead is one of the biggest time-savers. That's because these are often among the most time-consuming parts of a recipe, and may contain several different ingredients and require chopping. If you know that these completed components are already ready to go, it's a snap to pull together a meal or salad. Invest in small glass containers (mason jars work well for this) to store these items until they are ready to use. Most homemade dressings and sauces will stay fresh for up to one week if stored properly in your fridge. Also look for freezer-safe glass containers for storing items for longer periods.

One option I love is prepping all of my green smoothies and juices for the week; it helps me keep my daily green drink habit. Simply measure out the ingredients for a week's worth of green drinks, and then wash, chop, and bag them in individual portions. That way you can just grab a bag and the ingredients are ready to go into the juicer or blender. While this won't work well with some fruits, such as avocados and apples (as they go bad pretty quickly after they are cut), you can just wash them and cut them when it's time to make your drink.

As you get more experienced with meal prepping, feel free to add more items to your prep list. The great thing about prepping your meal ahead is that during the same amount of time that it takes for you to soak and cook beans, you can also cook the rice, quinoa, or lentils that you plan to eat during the week. While the burners are going, chop up your veggie sticks for the week, and consider washing and chopping additional vegetables that are going to be used in other recipes (such as onions, bell peppers, broccoli, and others that last a few days in the fridge after cutting).

Overall, remember to keep it simple or you could burn yourself out. Even if you just have time to prep one or two items, that will make the rest of the week a bit easier when you're in a time crunch. The ultimate goal is to prepare enough snacks and meal starters so that sticking to your healthy habits is a breeze.

I'm confident that meal planning is truly going to transform your health. It's time to stop outsourcing your food to the processed-food and restaurant industries to gain control of what you are putting into your body on a regular basis. You are well worth the effort!

THE BENEFITS OF EATING TOGETHER AS A FAMILY

Our family sits down together for dinner every evening at 5 p.m. We talk about our day, what we're excited about, and often make plans for the future. Most important, we never, ever, have a TV on. We focus on our food and the conversation. This is a special time that I look forward to every day! While this may seem old-fashioned to some, there are many amazing reasons why eating together as a family should become a priority in your life too.

For starters, children who regularly sit down to eat meals with their family tend to eat less processed foods and more fruits and vegetables.[2] You'll set your child up with healthier eating habits that they'll take with them into adulthood. This is an incredible benefit on its own, but there's more. It's been shown these children often have better communication skills, a healthier body weight,[3] higher self-esteem,[4] and even get better grades in school. One study found that dinnertime conversation improves the vocabulary of young children even more than reading books to them![5] Another study found that teens who eat with their family at least five times a week were twice as likely to get A's in school than teens who ate together fewer than twice per week.[6] And possibly the greatest benefit of all, eating together helps build strong relationships. Children who grow up eating together with their families are typically closer and communicate more freely with each other. Is your mind blown yet? It's pretty amazing that all of these benefits can be had by simply sitting down together to do something we all do every day anyway . . . eat!

So, it's time to stop slamming down dinner in front of the TV and start eating together as a family. Here are some tips that can help:

- Schedule a set meal time on your calendar and try not to let events and activities interfere during this time. If necessary, it's okay to have your meal away from home as well. For instance, you can have a picnic outdoors together before a game or practice.

- Your meal together doesn't need to be dinner. Perhaps it's more feasible for your family to eat breakfast or lunch together. Find whichever meal works best; as long as you are all sitting down together for at least one meal per day you will reap the benefits.

- Set a rule that you will turn off the TV, laptops, and phones when you sit down for a meal. This includes banishing reading materials such as magazines— and no shuffling through your mail either. Use this time

to sit down with your family and connect while enjoying your food.

- When they are old enough, involve your children in meal planning, food shopping, and cooking. Even when they are as young as two, they can help assemble salads, wash vegetables, and add ingredients to a mixing bowl. This will build valuable skills and create more excitement about the homemade meals being served.

- Keep the conversation during family meals positive and encouraging, and don't use this time for discipline. Ask your children what good things happened during the day and share your own fun experiences. This will help your child feel heard, loved, and looking forward to this time together.

- Before you dig in, make a mental note not to hurry and to eat mindfully. This makes it easier for your body to break down and absorb nutrients, as the chewing action releases important digestive enzymes that are crucial in delivering key nutrients to your cells. Give yourself at least 20 minutes to eat, as that is about how long it takes for your body to register when you are full. If eating more slowly is difficult for you, let go of your fork or spoon between bites. This will help you get used to chewing longer and eating more slowly.

- Set your table to create a positive mood, such as adding colorful place mats and some fresh flowers. Use all your senses to appreciate what you are eating and notice the smells, textures, and colors on your plate. Meals are meant to be enjoyed with those you love!

HABITS TO ROCKET-BOOST YOUR HEALTH, BODY, AND MIND

Most people make resolutions at the start of a new year to get healthier and lose weight . . . and we've all seen the results. The gyms get CRAZY, wellness books jump to the top of bestseller lists, and people become radical in their diets. A lot of us start doing all sorts of things we don't intend on doing for the rest of our lives. This is where the problem lies.

Instead of doing something just because it's a new year or bathing-suit season, why not take it a step further and develop a healthy habit for the rest of your life? This might seem idealistic, but it's really not. Especially since your health should be your number one priority for the rest of your life. Period.

No matter what time of year it is, *now* is the right time to get started. There is no better time than the present for a vibrant, healthy life. I've personally incorporated the healthy habits articulated below into my life, and have seen my health skyrocket. Now, don't jump in with both feet and try everything at once, even if you are excited. Get started by reading through the following six healthy habits and choose the one that you will start immediately. After that habit has become a regular part of your life, add another habit, and so on. Remember, these are life-changing habits—not something that you intend to do just for a few months. After you see your health and body transform, you'll never want to stop.

Cooking with Harley

I love teaching Harley everything I know about food, and one of the ways I do that is to include her in just about everything I do in the kitchen. She has tried so many different vegetables that by age three she knows them by name and can recognize them when they are outside growing, much more than I knew as an adult. I can only hope these teachings about *real food* will inspire her to make healthy choices as she grows up. Of course I also take the time to teach her about processed ingredients; it's a much trickier conversation, but I know she's learning!

How to Make Your Morning Lemon Water

- **Prepare the night before:** Every night, fill your tea pot with filtered water and take one lemon from the fridge and place it on the counter. Place your cayenne pepper bottle on the counter along with a cup filled halfway with water next to your lemon.

- **As soon as you get up in the morning:** Turn your kettle on to heat up the water for a few minutes. Pour the heated kettle water into your cup that is already half full with room temperature water.

- **Add lemon and cayenne:** Using a lemon squeezer, squeeze one-half of the lemon into the water, then sprinkle with a dash of cayenne pepper (optional).

- **Sip and soothe:** Sip this mixture with a glass straw so that your teeth aren't exposed to the acid. Drink at least 12 ounces, followed by another 8 ounces of filtered plain water afterward, before you eat or drink anything else.

6 HEALTHY HABITS TO START NOW

Healthy Habit #1: Drink Warm Lemon Water with Cayenne Pepper First Thing in the Morning

Maintaining this daily habit has amazing health benefits. Imagine getting sick less, feeling lighter, having regular eliminations, clearer skin, more energy, and having a boost in your metabolism leading to weight loss over time. How does it work? Drinking lemon water on an empty stomach provides a super-stimulant to the liver, your main detoxifying organ in the body. Your liver will release uric acid and create bile to safely eliminate environmental and lifestyle toxins that would otherwise be trapped in your digestive system longer.[7] The liver is at its most active in the morning, and the lemon helps speed up the elimination of toxins. Don't be surprised if you have to go to the bathroom quickly; this indicates the habit is working.

As you may know, keeping your liver and digestive system clean and in optimal condition will help your body prevent diseases like cancer in the future. The liver has hundreds of vital functions that support health and a healthy liver can support clearer eyes, healthier skin, a better attitude, and a more balanced weight. Combining cayenne with lemon increases the detoxing effect and raises the temperature of your body, which increases your metabolism.[8] Drinking this combination each morning will cleanse your body every single day safely and naturally.

Healthy Habit #2: Eliminate Refined Sugar from Your Diet

Let me clarify: I am not asking you to eliminate every type of sugar from your diet. That would set anyone up for failure. This habit entails eliminating *refined* sugars, such as white sugar, brown sugar, high-fructose corn syrup, and corn syrup. Avoiding refined sugars made from cane, sugar beets, and corn—but still enjoying naturally occurring sugar (i.e., fruit) in moderation—is one of the keys to ultimate balance in your diet. The problem with eating refined sugar from cane, corn, or sugar beets vs. other sources of sugar is that refined sugar is acid forming in the body as it has been chemically stripped of its minerals. The natural minerals in whole foods are important for our body's ability to process nutrients and ultimately to keep our bodies alkaline. A body in an alkaline state is primed to avoid disease and a myriad of other ailments. Food Babe–approved sugar sources include organic fresh fruit, coconut palm sugar, raw honey, maple syrup, date sugar, and dried fruit. The key here is to still include those forms of sugar in your diet, as your body can easily assimilate them and they provide nutrients, minerals, and vitamins your body will use.

Healthy Habit #3: Fast Every Single Day

Say what? Fast every single day?! That's insanity, you might be thinking. But it's not—

especially when you are fasting for only half the day and most of that time you are asleep. To adopt this habit, you will go without food for at least 12 hours a day, from the time you eat your last meal until the time you "break" the "fast" with breakfast. It takes at least eight hours for your body to completely digest its meals from the day. If you add in another four hours to that time without introducing more food to digest, the body goes into detoxification mode and has more time to remove dead and dying cells from the body. During this "idle" time, the body also stimulates the development and regeneration of new cells. Aging occurs when more cells die than are being produced. Allowing your body sufficient time every single day to digest food, eliminate dying cells, and develop new cells is a habit that will get you closer to drinking straight out of the fountain of youth!

Healthy Habit #4: Enjoy a Green Drink Daily

By "green drink," I mean a smoothie or a juice made mostly from kale, romaine lettuce, spinach, and other leafy veggies. If you've never had a drink like this before, that might sound disgusting to you . . . but just hear me out. Leafy greens are some of the healthiest foods you can eat, and you can make them taste delicious when you use the right combination of ingredients.

A simple green drink is the best fast-food available, and having one daily is a superb way to add more veggies to your diet and provide your body a rich source of chlorophyll. I've found, too, that green drinks alleviate food cravings because they provide a burst of nutrition—one not usually present in the typical American diet. When your body doesn't get what it needs nutritionally speaking, cravings kick in. And if you give in to those cravings, you're on the road to gaining weight. Once you start to pump your body with greens, you'll start craving them instead.

To make green juice, you use a juicer to extract the pulp/fiber from the produce, while a blender is used to make a smoothie (leaving the fiber intact). Having access to both green juices and green smoothies is important in one's quest for wellness and vitality. I drink both types of green drinks for different reasons. I drink juice to deliver as many nutrients to my body as possible at once, and I drink green smoothies for

Three Ways to Make a Green Drink

- **Make a green juice:** When juice is separated from the fiber of fruits and vegetables, it is easier for your body to absorb all the nutrients, giving you an instant boost of energy. If you're trying to drop pounds but you've got hard-to-control food cravings, it might be because your body is deficient in some vitamins and minerals; drinking green juice replenishes those elements and zaps your cravings to help you lose weight. All you need is a good juicer and a batch of organically grown fruits and vegetables. When juicing, it is very important to remember to keep the fruit juice component to a minimum—my general rule is either no fruit at all or one fruit per 12 ounces of green juice. You'll find my favorite juice recipes in chapter 4.

- **Make a green smoothie:** Depending on the types of fruits or vegetables you toss into your smoothie, you'll get a healthy, hefty dose of fiber, vitamins, minerals, live enzymes, and phytonutrients. All of these nutrients boost your antioxidant intake and enhance your body's natural detoxification process. Simply take a handful of leafy greens and throw them right into your blender along with a bit of frozen fruit (usually berries) and some good fat and protein (like chia and hemp seeds). You'll find my favorite smoothie recipes in chapter 4.

- **Make a wheatgrass shot:** The simplest way to have a green drink is to knock back a shot of wheatgrass juice. But let me warn you, it's going to be strong in taste, so it's not for the faint of heart. However, wheatgrass is one of the best sources of living chlorophyll available. Having a mere ounce of wheatgrass is the nutritional equivalent of eating two pounds of dark green leafy vegetables!

the beneficial fiber. As long as you chew your green drinks, your body will be able to digest and receive the benefits. It's important to swish around the juice or smoothie in your mouth or move your jaw up and down for a couple of seconds before swallowing to release your saliva, which contains important digestive enzymes that are crucial in delivering key nutrients to your cells. So don't just slam down a smoothie or juice—you need that chewing action for digestive enzymes to do their magic! Your daily green drink can be as simple as a wheatgrass shot or as big as a 32-ounce green smoothie packed with superfoods. It's your choice.

Healthy Habit #5: Change Your Grocery Store

Changing my grocery store has been fundamental in changing my health for the better. Typical large wholesale stores and conventional supermarkets are stocked with so many bad chemicals and ingredients it can make your head spin. The big food companies have created so many products that are full of anything but real food that it's probably cheaper for them to make these additive-filled foods than to use real, whole, and nutritious ingredients.

I understand that some big-name conventional grocery stores are making an

Ask for what you want: Contact your local grocery stores

Every purchase counts. In order to survive, food companies have to keep an eye on their bottom line. When we vote with our dollars, we send clear messages about what we want to see more of, and what we are not willing to support. If there is anything on this list that your local grocery stores do not carry, I encourage you to talk to them and request that they do.

In developing a relationship with the management at your grocery store, you can dramatically change the food options that they stock. They want to please us; they want to fill their shelves with the products that we will buy—otherwise food gets wasted and they lose money. The simple act of asking your local grocery store to carry more organic and healthy brands can make a huge improvement in the type of food that is available for you and your entire community to buy.

Drop off a letter to your local grocery store asking for better options or simply call or talk to the store manager. A carefully crafted letter will receive the most attention from management, and may be forwarded on, which can create even bigger changes. Remember to be specific about what brands and products you'd like them to carry.

Here's a sample letter to send to your local grocery store (for a printable version, visit FoodBabe.com/resources). You can use this one, editing it to remove the brands your store already carries or writing in additional brands you like:

Dear _____ [fill in store manager name]:

I am writing to you as one of your regular customers to thank you for the selection of certified organic and healthy products that are currently on your shelves. As certified organic products have become a larger share of the market, desired by many people such as myself, I would like to ask you to expand this selection.

Below please find a quick list of products that I would like to purchase in your store. As an increasing amount of retailers across the country are open to special requests such as this for new products, I am hopeful that these products can find a place on the shelves in your store. Thank you for being open to these requests.

Here are some suggested options for great brands that are found all over the country at local grocery stores just like ours:

- **Milk/Yogurt:** local and organic; Organic Valley Grass-milk; Traders Point Creamery; MALK nut milks; Maple Hill Creamery

- **Chicken/Beef:** local and organic; White Oak Pastures; Organic Prairie; Jones Creek; Thousand Hills Farm; Hearst Ranch

- **Bread:** Ezekiel; Food For Life; Dave's Killer Bread

- **Juice:** raw, organic, and cold-pressed; Uncle Matt's Organic; Lakewood Organic

- **Cereal:** Ezekiel; Purely Elizabeth; Go Raw

- **Pasta:** Tolerant lentil pasta; Jovial einkorn pasta

- **Eggs:** local and organic; Vital Farms; The Country Hen; Organic Valley organic brown eggs

- **Cooking Oil:** organic, cold-pressed coconut oil; ghee; olive oil

- **Protein Powder:** Truvani

- **Produce:** local and organic; (Next Best: organic frozen veggies)

- **Sugar and Snacks:** coconut sugar; Late July Snacks; Jackson's Honest chips; Mary's Gone Crackers snacks; 479° Popcorn; Coconut Bliss ice cream; Madhava sprouted brownie or cookie mix; organic dried fruit

Thank you for taking the time to address my concerns and for taking a step in the right direction to provide safe, clean food for my family and me while supporting local producers and a healthier planet.

Sincerely,
[Name]
[Phone Number]

effort to include more organic produce and organic convenience foods, but they still carry all the chemical-laden foods too. This makes shopping there 10 times harder because, unless you know the brand and trust it, it means reading lots of labels and deciphering chemical names of ingredients. Instead, look for local health food stores and alternative grocery stores in your town. Some stores now ban certain ingredients from ever hitting their shelves, such really serious ingredients as growth hormones in dairy products that are known to cause cancer, and high-fructose corn syrup that is linked to diabetes and obesity.

Depending on where you live and the time of year, you may not even need to go into a grocery store at all on a regular basis—you can go to the farmers market to get local and organic produce or grow your own food as much as possible. And sometimes you don't even need to leave your house. Buying organic staples from Internet sources is a terrific way to save money and time. For instance, I can buy organic coconut palm sugar online for about half the price as in most natural-food stores. This can add up to big savings over time and is well worth the click. I also buy coconut oil, Ezekiel tortillas, nuts, dried fruit, and various organic snacks on the Internet. Support establishments that want you to do well! Vote with your dollars. And shop smart.

Healthy Habit #6:
Stop Drinking with Your Meals

When you drink a lot of water with your meals, you dilute your naturally occurring di-gestive enzymes and stomach acids, which makes it harder for your body to break down food. Stomach acids are dissipated with the act of consuming liquids with solids because water is excreted faster than solids. If you are chewing adequately (creating saliva), you should be able to eat comfortably without supplementary liquids. Allow your saliva to help you swallow your food naturally.

Focus on hydrating yourself between, instead of during, meals by drinking water or other liquids 20 minutes before and at least an hour after you consume food. You'll still be adequately hydrated throughout the day and allow your food to be digested properly.

Digestion is super important for health, staying slim, and mental well-being. Without proper digestion many discomforts can be born into the body—indigestion, heartburn, irritability, bloating, lethargy, headaches, insatiable cravings, inability to determine true hunger, and depression. While eating, you want all your energy directed at breaking down food so your body can easily assimi-late the nutrients and eliminate waste. When you have bad digestion you could actually gain weight in the long run, because toxins can be built up in your digestive organs and inhibit the body's ability to break down fat while causing insatiable cravings and mess-ing with your body's ability to determine whether or not it is full.

If you must drink with your meals, sip on a warm beverage. Good options are room temperature water with lemon, or herbal tea—the temperature will be closer to your body's normal heat and ease digestion ver-sus disrupting it. Ginger is my favorite type of tea to drink with or after meals because it naturally moves food from the upper part of the digestive tract into the lower. To make ginger tea, simply cut up a few pieces of fresh ginger and pour hot water over it.

LET THE FUN BEGIN!

Now that you've got your kitchen stocked with all the healthy essentials and have your habits in check, it's time to move on to the fun part. Let's get cooking! Which recipe are you going to try first? If you find it hard to decide, I'd start with one of the breakfast recipes. This way you'll set yourself up for the day with a fantastic, nutrient-dense meal.

And I'd love to see your favorites. Please post pictures of your amazing meals on social media using the hashtag #FoodBabeKitchen. I can't wait to see what you're loving and making!

Avoiding Processed Food

As you start paying close attention to ingredient lists, you'll notice that the majority of packaged products on the grocery store shelves are made from primarily white/beige foods (wheat, soy, sugar, corn) which have been stripped of their natural nutrients and artificially colored, flavored, and fortified with vitamins and minerals to resemble "food." These products are not real food at all—and your body can really tell the difference.

I know this firsthand, as my health improved dramatically when I changed my eating habits and started filling my body with raw whole foods from all the colors of the rainbow: leafy greens, red beets, orange carrots, purple cabbage, blueberries . . . as varied a selection as possible. Eating an abundance of raw and colorful food, and avoiding most processed food, is one of the habits I live by. Eat the rainbow!

The absolute best thing about eating this way is that your food hasn't been adulterated with artificial colors, flavors, chemicals, pesticides, additives, preservatives, or BPA and other harmful packaging materials. Plus, it's a great way to ensure that you are giving your body what it needs. So don't forget to eat the rainbow today and every day. And I don't mean Skittles!

PART II

LET'S GET COOKING!

chapter 3

MORNINGS

Mornings are busy and I don't want to spend the whole time cooking, so I make a lot of meals on lazy weekends and freeze them for busy weekdays. In our family, we have some long-standing favorites (like Harley's Blueberry Zucchini Muffins), which are great to make as a big batch and freeze to warm up at breakfast time. This works for pancakes and waffles too.

SWEET POTATO WAFFLES
with Cinnamon Whipped Butter

There is something glorious about Sunday mornings enjoying these waffles. This recipe uses oat flour, which is an amazing substitute if you are trying to eat gluten-free and/or consume fewer wheat products. You can simply buy oat flour or grind your own from steel-cut or rolled oats in a blender for a few seconds. In less than 20 minutes you'll have sweet golden waffles! Yum. To make the flavorful whipped butter, scrape the seeds from a split vanilla bean using the back of a knife, or for an easy substitute, use vanilla extract. The waffle recipe doubles easily if serving a larger group.

Makes 3 to 4 servings (3 to 4 waffles)
Prep Time: 10 minutes
Cook Time: 10 minutes

1 cup oat flour
3 tablespoons coconut sugar
1 tablespoon baking powder
½ teaspoon ground cinnamon
½ teaspoon sea salt
1 cup diced peeled sweet potato, roasted and mashed
2 tablespoons coconut oil, melted
⅓ cup coconut milk (or more, as needed)
2 large eggs, separated
Maple syrup for serving (optional)

CINNAMON WHIPPED BUTTER

¼ cup butter, softened
½ teaspoon ground cinnamon
½ teaspoon vanilla bean seeds or vanilla extract
Pinch of sea salt

Heat and grease a waffle iron.

Mix together the flour, sugar, baking powder, cinnamon, and salt in a large bowl.

Add the mashed sweet potato, oil, ⅓ cup milk, and egg yolks. Whisk to combine, adding more milk by tablespoons if very thick.

Beat the egg whites in a medium bowl until stiff peaks form, then fold the egg whites into the batter.

Drop roughly ½ to ¾ cup batter onto your waffle iron and cook until golden brown.

To make the Cinnamon Whipped Butter, place all the ingredients in a bowl and whisk vigorously.

Serve the waffles with a dollop of the butter and a drizzle of maple syrup, if desired.

BANANA NUT OVERNIGHT OATS

This is the ultimate make-ahead, healthy, on-the-go breakfast or snack. I love having something yummy ready and easy to eat on busy mornings. You can make this up to three days in advance and multiply the recipe to stock up your fridge. For variety, you can top your oats with virtually whatever fruit you like—instead of banana, try some berries!

Makes 2 to 3 servings
Prep Time: 5 minutes plus overnight

1¼ cups rolled oats
1¼ cups almond or coconut milk
1 ripe banana, peeled and mashed
½ cup plain yogurt
¼ cup chopped walnuts
1 scoop Truvani protein powder
1 tablespoon chia seeds
1 teaspoon vanilla extract
½ teaspoon ground cinnamon
¼ teaspoon sea salt

Optional Toppings

Sliced bananas
Chopped walnuts
Unsweetened coconut flakes

Place all the ingredients in a jar and mix well to combine. Place in the refrigerator overnight to set.

Serve with desired toppings.

HARLEY'S BLUEBERRY ZUCCHINI MUFFINS

I always have a batch of these blueberry zucchini muffins ready in the freezer for a quick snack or to add to Harley's meals. They take just minutes to thaw in a toaster oven, and she loves them! They are super moist, taste absolutely delicious, and are perfect for both kids and adults. The best part? They have no added sugar. I try to give Harley vegetables with every meal, and thankfully she loves them. If your kids aren't veggie lovers yet, the zucchini in these muffins is a great way to sneak some in; they won't even know they are there.

1½ cups oat flour
1 teaspoon ground cinnamon
1 teaspoon baking soda
½ teaspoon sea salt
¼ teaspoon baking powder
2 large eggs
½ cup unsweetened apple sauce
1 ripe banana, peeled and mashed
⅓ cup butter or coconut oil, melted
1 cup grated zucchini
½ cup wild frozen blueberries, thawed

Makes 36 mini muffins or 12 large muffins
Prep Time: 15 minutes
Cook Time: 10 to 12 minutes for mini muffins;
18 minutes for large muffins

Preheat the oven to 350°F.

Place the dry ingredients in a bowl and mix to combine.

Mix together the wet ingredients in a separate bowl. Slowly add the dry ingredients to the wet ingredients and mix until just combined. Fold in the zucchini and blueberries.

Line mini-muffin pans or standard muffin cups with liners or grease with coconut oil. Fill each opening ¾ way full. Place the pans in the oven and bake until a tester inserted into the center of a muffin comes out clean, about 10 to 12 minutes for mini muffins and 18 minutes for large muffins.

You can store extra muffins in the freezer, reheating in a toaster oven or standard oven, or place them in your fridge the day before you want to eat them so they can thaw overnight.

CREAMY PUMPKIN SPICE QUINOA PORRIDGE

Imagine all the flavors of pumpkin pie in a big, hot bowl of goodness—that's what this breakfast is. It might as well be a dessert, it tastes that good! Fortunately, this porridge will give you staying power, a nice dose of healthy fiber, and disease-busting nutrients without the sugar high.

Makes 2 servings
Prep Time: 5 minutes
Cook Time: 16 to 18 minutes

1½ cups unsweetened almond milk or coconut milk, divided
1 cup dry quinoa, rinsed and drained
½ cup pumpkin puree
1 teaspoon ground cinnamon
½ teaspoon ground ginger
⅛ teaspoon ground cloves
¼ teaspoon sea salt
2 tablespoons ground flaxseed
3 tablespoons maple syrup

Optional Toppings

Chopped walnuts
Coconut flakes
Diced apples
Golden raisins

Heat 1 cup of water and 1 cup of almond milk in a heavy medium saucepan over medium-high heat. Bring to a boil, then add the quinoa, pumpkin puree, cinnamon, ginger, cloves, and salt. Reduce the heat and simmer, stirring occasionally, for 16 to 18 minutes or until the liquid has evaporated and the porridge thickens.

Take the pan off the heat and stir in the ground flaxseed.

Serve with the remaining ½ cup almond milk, maple syrup, and desired toppings. The porridge can be made 3 days ahead and refrigerated. Reheat in a saucepan over medium heat, adding enough water to loosen, and stirring often.

MORNING POTATO BAKE

There's nothing quite like a hearty Sunday brunch with these breakfast potatoes. Instead of frying them in a pan, which takes *forever* and uses a ton of oil, I simply bake them in the oven. This allows me to spend less time in the kitchen and more time with the family on lazy weekend mornings. I like to prepare all the ingredients the night before, storing them in a bowl before throwing them onto a big pan in the morning. Try topping these with some avocado slices, or maybe a fried egg—it's so, so good.

Makes 4 servings
Prep Time: 10 minutes
Cook Time: 25 to 30 minutes

1 tablespoon coconut oil, melted
½ cup diced yellow onion
1 garlic clove, minced
1 green bell pepper, diced
1 red bell pepper, diced
2 small sweet or russet potatoes, peeled and diced
¼ teaspoon chili powder
¼ teaspoon sea salt
fresh ground pepper, to taste
1 tablespoon fresh chopped parsley
1 avocado, peeled and sliced (optional)

Preheat the oven to 375°F.

Place all ingredients except parsley and avocado into a large bowl, and toss to combine.

Place mixture onto a sheet pan lined with a silpat or parchment paper, and bake for 25 to 30 minutes or until potatoes are tender and crispy.

Top with chopped parsley and sliced avocado, if desired, and serve.

SLOW COOKER STEEL-CUT OATS

This is my go-to breakfast recipe that my entire family eats almost every weekday morning. Not only do steel-cut oats make a filling and healthy breakfast, but they are also easy to prepare ahead of time so that you don't need to cook in the morning. These creamy oats take less than a minute to prep at night before bed. Compare this to making oats in the morning while you're busy and waiting 30 or more minutes for them to cook, watching the stove, and stirring, or even worse, resorting to instant oats that are not as nutritious. Keep in mind that it is vital to use a small (1.5 quart) slow cooker for this recipe; otherwise your oats may burn. If you plan to make this as often as I do, a small slow cooker is worth the investment (unless you have a large family and need to make more servings).

Makes 4 servings
Prep Time: 2 minutes
Cook Time: overnight

1 cup steel-cut oats

Optional Toppings

Freshly ground flaxseed
Chia seeds
Fresh berries
Sliced peaches

Place the oats and 4½ cups filtered water in a small, 1.5-quart slow cooker.

Turn the heat to low and cook for at least 8 hours or overnight. Serve with a variety of healthful toppings.

TURKEY AND RED PEPPER EGG "MUFFINS"

This is one of my daughter's favorite breakfasts. I like to cook up several portions and freeze them to heat up quickly on busy mornings. These egg muffins also make a great addition to brunch with the family alongside a platter of fresh fruit and some organic croissants. Yum!

Makes 2 to 4 servings (8 "muffins")
Prep Time: 10 minutes
Cook Time: 18 to 20 minutes

5 large eggs
1 cup cooked ground turkey
½ red bell pepper, diced
½ small yellow onion, diced
¼ teaspoon red pepper flakes
¼ teaspoon paprika
¼ teaspoon sea salt
Ground black pepper, to taste
½ teaspoon coconut oil or olive oil (to coat muffin tin, or use baking cups)

Preheat the oven to 375°F.

Place all the ingredients except the coconut oil in a large bowl and mix well to combine.

Grease a standard muffin tin with the coconut oil, or line with paper baking cups. Pour the mixture into the muffin cups, using about ⅓ cup of mixture for each.

Bake until the mixture is set in the center and the tops of the muffins are golden, about 18 to 20 minutes. Let rest for at least 5 minutes before serving. Run a small knife around the muffins to loosen, or use a large spoon to scoop the egg muffins from the pan.

EASY GRANOLA CEREAL

This superfood cereal is easy to store and makes a great replacement for the sugary processed cereals available for purchase. It will keep for up to two weeks, although it never lasts that long in my house. You can serve this cereal simply with some nut milk, or layer it into a yogurt parfait with fresh fruit (see page 79).

Makes 4 cups
Prep Time: 10 minutes
Cook Time: 20 minutes

3 cups rolled oats

2 cups raw nuts of your choice, chopped

¾ cup shredded unsweetened coconut

3 tablespoons chia seeds

1 tablespoon vanilla extract

¼ cup coconut oil, melted

⅓ cup raw honey

¾ teaspoon sea salt

2 teaspoons ground cinnamon

¾ cup dried goji berries

Preheat the oven to 250°F.

Combine all the ingredients except for the goji berries and mix well.

Place the mixture on a parchment-lined baking sheet.

Bake for 1 hour, stirring every 20 minutes.

Remove the granola from the oven and let cool. Stir in the goji berries.

The granola can be stored in an airtight container for up to 2 weeks.

MY MOM'S HOMEMADE YOGURT

The food industry has a reputation for taking incredibly healthy items and turning them into processed junk food—and this is exactly what has happened to most yogurts on the market. That's why I feel incredibly fortunate that my mother makes me her homemade yogurt, so I don't have to buy it very often. She has been making this yogurt for as long as I can remember! I will pass this down to my own daughter as well. I start with the best ingredients, of course—organic grass-fed (and raw, if you can find it) milk is ideal.

Makes 4 to 6 servings
Prep Time: 10 minutes plus 10 hours to set

4 cups organic grass-fed milk
3 tablespoons plain organic yogurt
or powdered yogurt starter

Heat the milk in a pot over medium heat until it starts to bubble, stirring constantly to prevent skin from forming.

Cool the milk until it is lukewarm (about 110°F to 115°F).

Add the organic yogurt or yogurt starter to the milk and stir together. Pour the mixture into small glass jars or one large glass container.

Place lids on the jars, put a towel over them, and store in a draft-free place at room temperature for 6 to 8 hours.

Set the yogurt in the fridge for at least 2 hours before serving. The yogurt can be stored in the fridge for up to 1 week.

HOMEMADE YOGURT PARFAITS

These parfaits are somewhat fancy-looking and perfect for company when you don't have a lot of time to spend in the kitchen. I love to serve them with long spoons in tall clear glasses so you can see all the pretty layers. This makes them fun to eat too!

Makes 2 servings
Prep Time: 5 minutes

1 cup Easy Granola Cereal (page 75)
1 cup My Mom's Homemade Yogurt (page 76)
1 cup fresh berries or sliced fruit of choice

Place ¼ cup of granola in a glass. Layer ¼ cup of yogurt on top, followed by ¼ cup of fruit. Repeat to form 6 layers total for each serving.

BLUEBERRY CINNAMON FRENCH TOAST BAKE

French toast is usually made with inferior white bread, a lot of butter, heavy cream, and sugar. This casserole version is completely clean, has a beautiful crunch, and uses healthy sprouted grain bread. It's the perfect make-ahead breakfast when you have company staying with you as it will feed a crowd and you don't need to spend hours in the kitchen. Simply assemble it the evening before bed—and then in the morning you can sit back and relax with your loved ones while breakfast is quietly baking in the oven.

Makes 6 servings
Prep Time: 10 minutes
Cook Time: 40 minutes

6 eggs
1½ cups almond milk
1 tablespoon vanilla extract
¼ teaspoon sea salt
¼ teaspoon ground nutmeg
1 teaspoon ground cinnamon
10 slices sprouted grain bread
1½ cups fresh blueberries
½ cup toasted walnuts, chopped
Maple syrup and coconut oil/butter to serve

Beat the eggs, milk, vanilla, sea salt, nutmeg, and cinnamon together.

Grease a 9-inch baking dish with butter or coconut oil.

Place 5 slices of bread in the dish in a single layer, breaking up pieces to fit in every nook and cranny. Top the bread with half of the egg mixture.

Layer ¼ cup of walnuts and half of the blueberries on top. Repeat this process once more.

Cover and refrigerate overnight or for at least 8 hours. In the morning, preheat the oven to 350°F. Bake covered for 30 to 40 minutes. Serve with hot maple syrup or butter.

BISCUITS
with Whipped Honey Butter

If there are biscuits on the table, oh am I in trouble . . . I love them so much. However, you'll never find me buying those blue cans of premade biscuit dough. Those little puppies aren't even made with butter. Instead they use refined soybean oils mixed with emulsifiers and artificial flavors along with risky preservatives like TBHQ. No thanks! I found a way to make biscuits healthier by using sprouted flour, grass-fed milk, and, of course, real grass-fed butter. Bake these when you want to impress someone. I mean, who doesn't love homemade biscuits? Bonus: As kids love playing with dough and flour, this is a great recipe to make as a family.

Makes 10 large biscuits or 18 small biscuits
Prep Time: 10 minutes
Cook Time: 18 minutes

2 cups sprouted whole wheat
or spelt flour
1 tablespoon baking powder
1 teaspoon sea salt
½ cup (1 stick) chilled unsalted butter
cut into ½-inch pieces
½ cup grass-fed milk

WHIPPED
HONEY BUTTER

½ cup (1 stick) salted butter
2 tablespoons raw honey

Preheat the oven to 425°F.

Mix together the flour, baking powder, and salt in a medium bowl.

Add the butter and cut in with a pastry cutter or back of a fork until the mixture resembles coarse meal.

Slowly add the milk and mix until the dough begins to come together into a ball.

Roll the dough out on a floured surface to a thickness of ½ inch. Cut out biscuits using a 2½-inch round cutter for large biscuits, and a 2-inch round cutter for small biscuits.

Place the biscuits on a parchment-lined baking sheet and bake for 15 minutes or until golden brown.

While the biscuits are baking, make the honey butter: Beat the butter and honey together in a small bowl until well combined.

Serve the biscuits warm with the honey butter.

FLUFFY MAPLE BANANA PANCAKES

These fluffy pancakes are super filling and comforting on a rainy morning. I serve them with real maple syrup and fresh berries on top. This recipe is written to be generous enough for leftovers on purpose, because they freeze wonderfully. I stack the extras with a little piece of parchment paper in between, and throw them in the freezer. I then thaw one out at a time, for Harley on busy mornings.

Makes 4 servings (12 pancakes or 24 mini pancakes)
Prep Time: 10 minutes
Cook Time: 10 minutes

2 cups blanched almond flour
2 teaspoons baking powder
½ teaspoon sea salt
1 ripe banana, peeled and mashed
4 large eggs, beaten
2 tablespoons melted coconut oil
2 teaspoons vanilla extract
1 tablespoon grass-fed butter

Optional Toppings

Butter
Maple syrup
Fresh fruit

Mix together flour, baking powder, and salt and set aside.

In a separate large bowl, place the mashed banana, eggs, coconut oil, and vanilla extract and whisk to combine. Slowly stir dry ingredients into wet ingredients.

Heat a griddle with butter over medium heat. Working in batches, add the pancake batter by 2 tablespoonfuls, spreading slightly with the back of the spoon and cooking until bubbles form and pop on the surface, about 1 minute. Using a spatula, flip the pancakes over and cook until they're brown on the bottom, about 1 minute. Add more butter to the griddle between batches as needed.

Serve with toppings as desired.

ACAI BERRY BOWL

When we were on a small island called Parrot Cay in Turks and Caicos, the resort offered this fabulous acai bowl for breakfast every morning. It was so good, Harley and I ordered it every day for a week. When we got home, I knew I needed to re-create the goodness. I love having fruit first thing in the morning. It's so refreshing and energizing.

Makes 1 serving
Prep Time: 5 minutes

1 cup fresh berries of choice
(quartered strawberries, blueberries,
raspberries, etc.)
100-gram packet frozen acai
½ frozen ripe banana, cut into
4 pieces
2 tablespoons or more liquid of
choice (water, nut milk, coconut
milk, etc.)

Optional Toppings
Granola
Fresh fruit
Chopped nuts
Seeds

Place the berries, acai, banana, and 2 tablespoons liquid in a blender and blend until smooth, stopping occasionally to scrape down sides; or use a tamper/plunger to help blend the ingredients together. Add more liquid by tablespoons as necessary to form a thick, stiff puree.

Pour the mixture into a bowl and sprinkle with your desired toppings.

Spruce Up Your Coffee *without* Sugar

Do you eat a healthy diet, but still run by a coffee shop to pick up a vanilla latte on the way to work? Do you reward yourself with a mocha in the afternoon? Of course you know these coffee drinks contain sugar—but do you really know how much, and how that sugar is affecting your body? You might think twice about all the sugar in a donut or a candy bar, but what about what's in your coffee?

Keep this in mind next time you crave a coffee drink: Just one drink from Starbucks can contain 11 teaspoons of sugar, which is more than a can of Coke. If you crash and burn from the sugar rush later, don't say I didn't warn you. Instead of jacking up your blood sugar every time you drink a cup, try stirring these into your coffee and feel the difference in your health:

CINNAMON Putting cinnamon in your coffee adds a hint of sweetness and also provides the immune system with a boost, which we can all use in the morning! I just sprinkle a little bit on top, but some people stir it into the grounds before brewing, or put a cinnamon stick into the brewed coffee. If you would like to vary the flavor, try nutmeg or cardamom.

NUT MILK, COCONUT MILK, OR COCONUT CREAM This is a great way to add an instant, full-bodied feel to your coffee. Coconut is naturally sweet and will sweeten your coffee without refined sugar. I like to treat my homemade coconut milk to a milk frother before adding it to my coffee (and then topping the whole thing with cinnamon). The frother really helps to add creaminess—you'll never miss those dairy creamers! For extra flavor, try adding a bit of vanilla extract to the coconut or nut milk to create your own homemade dairy-free vanilla creamer. You can also use dried coconut milk on the go or while traveling.

UNSWEETENED COCOA OR CACAO POWDER Mixing chocolate with coffee enhances subtle notes in the beans that you may not have noticed before. Cacao has also been shown to provide important antioxidants, which can increase the overall quality of your morning coffee. Stir a small amount into the brewed coffee, or into the grounds before brewing.

VANILLA EXTRACT OR ALMOND EXTRACT These naturally sweet extracts are an amazing way to wean yourself off using added sugar or sweeteners. Just stir in a couple of drops.

GRASS-FED BUTTER AND COCONUT OIL While adding butter to your coffee may sound odd to you, the effect of adding a healthy fat such as coconut oil to your coffee creates a fullness that also helps your energy levels. Grass-fed butter and/or coconut oil will add natural creaminess, especially when blended into your coffee with a hand blender or frother (don't just stir it in), and make sure to use organic unsalted grass-fed butter. A tablespoon of coconut oil by itself is also used to fight off cravings, especially for sugar.

TRUVANI MARINE COLLAGEN You won't taste it, but your health will thank you. Cutting-edge research suggests that getting more collagen into your system promotes youthful-looking skin, healthy hair, and stronger nails, and provides support to your body's connective tissues and joints. There's no easier way to take this supplement than by stirring a scoop into your morning coffee. A frother comes in handy here too!

SEA SALT It may seem counterintuitive, but did you know that adding a pinch of sea salt to a pot of coffee can help enhance its natural sweetness? Salt reduces bitterness, so your coffee will seem sweeter without any sugar. Just be sure to add only a little pinch (either to the grounds before brewing or to the entire pot); don't go overboard or your coffee will taste salty! I like to use this tip along with one of the other options above.

If you are used to the hyper-sweetened drinks from coffee shops, these alternatives might take a little bit of time to get used to. But I know from personal experience that once you start implementing healthier substitutes your body will start to crave them—and the cravings for sugar will fade away.

chapter 4

DRINKS, SHAKES, AND SMOOTHIES

I often get asked, Which is better, a fresh juice or a smoothie?
My answer is . . . both! They are both important in your quest for wellness
and vitality. I drink juice to deliver as many nutrients to my body as possible—
which gives me a ton of energy. I drink green smoothies for the beneficial fiber
and to increase the amount of vegetables (especially dark leafy greens) I am eating
per day. I also love making smoothies for fast food. If I don't have time to cook or
prepare food, a green smoothie with additional enhancements like Truvani protein
powder, hemp seeds, chia seeds, or pumpkin seeds makes a great meal replacement.

TURMERIC COOLER

I need to tell you that juicing turmeric can be really tricky. If you use too much, the juice can end up very bitter and not at all pleasant to drink. I experimented with a few different blends that don't use fruit juice or sugar (as most recipes call for) because I wanted to find a way to drink this all the time without having to consume the added sugar. This blend is so refreshing; the coolness of the cucumber and romaine work like a charm. I hope you can find fresh turmeric root wherever you are, because this juice is the BOMB.

Makes 2 servings
Prep Time: 15 minutes

2-inch piece of turmeric
1 bunch of romaine lettuce
3 carrots
1 lemon, peel removed
1 cucumber, ends removed

Wash all the vegetables thoroughly and place them in a large bowl.

Juice each vegetable in this order: turmeric, romaine, carrots, lemon, and cucumber.

Stir before serving. Clean your juicer immediately.

How to Make Juice
without a Juicer (It's so Easy!)

I had a blender many years before I had a juicer. I know investing in a new kitchen appliance can be tough, especially if you are new to juicing, so I'm taking the opportunity to share this simple technique with you. This method works great for times when you don't have access to a juicer, such as while traveling. I don't know many people who travel with their juicers—those luggage fees are crazy and we need the extra room for shoes, right?

Below are step-by-step instructions for how to juice without a juicer: All you need are the vegetables and fruits you want to juice, a fine-mesh strainer or nut-milk bag, and a high-powered blender.

- **Step 1: Prepare Your Produce** Clean your organic fruits and vegetables thoroughly and cut them up into pieces. I like to completely submerge my leafy greens in water and let the dirt and sediment fall to the bottom of the bowl, and then rinse the greens twice more with fresh filtered water.

- **Step 2: Blend Your Greens** If there are leafy greens in your juice, you will want to blend them first. Add a few tablespoons of water to a clean blender, then the juice of one lemon (if this is part of the recipe), and then slowly add the leafy greens before the rest of your ingredients. I find that blending the greens first produces the best result (you only need to blend them for about 30 seconds).

- **Step 3: Add Additional Fruits and Vegetables** Add other fruits and vegetables and blend well for about 1 or 2 minutes.

- **Step 4: Strain Your Juice** Strain the mixture through a fine-mesh strainer or through a nut-milk bag for a less pulpy, silky smooth result. (Tip: You may find it less messy to strain the mixture into a large bowl first, instead of directly into a glass.)

To get the most nutrition out of it, enjoy your beautiful green juice immediately.

HOMEMADE GINGER ALE

When I realized that store-bought ginger ale is usually made with no real ginger, I was so disgusted. Manufacturers use "natural flavors" instead, because it is cheaper than using real ginger. That's why I came up with this recipe for fresh homemade ginger ale. It's sweet, spicy, and sooooo refreshing on a hot day. My family goes bonkers for this drink.

Makes 1 serving
Prep Time: 10 minutes

2-inch piece fresh ginger root, juiced
12 ounces sparkling water
1 squeeze fresh lemon
2 tablespoons raw honey or maple syrup

Combine all the ingredients. Serve over ice.

Tip: *If you don't have a juicer, you can blend the ginger with the lemon juice and squeeze the juice out of a cheese cloth or fine mesh strainer.*

GOLDEN MILK LATTE

This soothing drink is perfect before bedtime. It's really relaxing and helps to take the edge off a hard day. I like to drink my golden milk like a little dessert after dinner, so I add maple syrup—but you can skip that, or use coconut sugar or honey instead. Any of those would be delicious. One reason we developed Truvani Turmeric in an uncoated tablet was so that we could easily use it in recipes like this, with no mess! If you've ever accidentally spilled turmeric powder on your counter, you know what I mean. If you don't have Truvani Turmeric tablets on hand, go ahead and use a teaspoon of organic ground turmeric in this recipe. To experience all the healing benefits, it's super important to use only high-quality organic turmeric.

Makes 2 servings
Prep Time: 5 minutes
Cook Time: 10 minutes

1¾ cups coconut or almond milk (one 13.5-ounce can)

3 Truvani Turmeric tablets or 1 teaspoon turmeric powder

½ teaspoon ground cinnamon

¼ teaspoon ground ginger

1 to 2 tablespoons maple syrup or raw honey (optional)

Place all the ingredients in a small pot over medium-low heat.

Gently simmer for 8 to 10 minutes, stirring occasionally to dissolve the turmeric and combine the flavors.

NO-SUGAR
HOT CHOCOLATE

I love hot chocolate, but I hate the instant stuff you combine with hot water. Have you seen those ingredients? No thanks! Instead, I make this recipe. It's warm and comforting and with no added sugar.

Makes 2 servings
Prep Time: 5 minutes
Cook Time: 5 minutes

2½ cups almond milk or coconut milk
2 dates, pitted
4 tablespoons raw cacao powder
1 teaspoon vanilla extract
Pinch of sea salt

Combine all the ingredients in a blender and blend until smooth.

Transfer the liquid to a small pot and warm slowly to the desired temperature.

HARLEY'S FAVORITE SMOOTHIE

Harley loves the taste of this smoothie and I am so happy to get so much powerful raw kale into her diet each day. I freeze portions in little 4- or 8-ounce jars for her to have during the week, taking one out the night before or early in the morning to defrost while we get ready. You can pack these in lunch bags too, and they'll be the perfect consistency in a few hours. I've even packed these in a Yeti cooler in my checked luggage to have when I'm traveling.

Makes 4 to 6 servings
Prep Time: 5 minutes

3 cups kale, spinach, or romaine lettuce
1 frozen banana, peeled
1 cup frozen pineapple
1 cup frozen mango
4 tablespoons almond butter
2-inch piece fresh ginger root, chopped
8 ounces filtered water

Place all the ingredients in a blender and blend until smooth.

Tip: Peel a fresh banana and freeze in a freezer-safe container; you can also slice before freezing!

COCONUT MILK 3 WAYS

If you've ever picked up a box of coconut milk from the store and read the ingredients, it probably looked something like this: water, coconut cream, cane sugar, tricalcium phosphate, carrageenan, guar gum, coconut water concentrate, natural flavors . . . The list of ingredients in most store-bought coconut milk is absolutely ridiculous, especially since you need only two ingredients to make it: coconut and water! Let me show you three ways to make coconut milk with ingredients you probably already have in your pantry.

COCONUT MILK FROM A CAN

Makes 6 to 8 servings
Prep Time: 5 minutes

4 cups filtered water
One 13.5-ounce can coconut milk
(BPA-free)

Blend or shake really hard and serve.

COCONUT MILK FROM SHREDDED COCONUT

Makes 6 to 8 servings
Prep Time: 5 minutes

2 cups shredded unsweetened coconut
4 cups filtered water

Place the ingredients in a blender and blend on high for 1 to 2 minutes.

Strain through a nut-milk bag or fine-mesh strainer.

COCONUT MILK FROM COCONUT MANNA

Makes 6 to 8 servings
Prep Time: 5 minutes

1 cup coconut manna
(from one 15-ounce jar)
3 cups filtered water

Place the jar of coconut manna in a bowl of warm to hot water to allow the manna to soften.

When the manna is soft, add 1 cup to 3 cups filtered water in a blender and blend on medium speed until combined.

Strain through a nut-milk bag or fine-mesh strainer.

KICKIN' KALE JUICE

Kale is one of the things I would take with me on a deserted island. That's because it's one of the most powerful plant foods in the world, full of vitamins A, C, and B_6; manganese; calcium; copper; and potassium. Juicing kale unlocks even more power because your body is able to absorb the live enzymes and nutrients immediately. So here it is, my everyday recipe for kale juice. I drink some combination of this on most days of the week, frequently switching out different types of kale. The fresh ginger adds a nice kick!

Makes 2 servings
Prep Time: 10 minutes

1 bunch curly kale
½ bunch cilantro or parsley
½ bunch celery
2-inch piece fresh ginger root
1 cucumber, ends removed
1 lemon, peel removed
1 green apple (optional, for added sweetness)

Wash all the ingredients thoroughly and place them in a large bowl.

Juice each ingredient in this order: kale, cilantro, celery, ginger, cucumber, lemon, and apple, if using. Stir the mixture before serving and clean your juicer immediately.

GINGER GREEN SMOOTHIE

One of the most powerful anti-inflammatory foods is ginger. That's why throwing a big hunk of ginger into your daily green smoothies is the best idea ever, and perfect after a workout. If you are battling an ailment, or just want to feel good, this smoothie rocks. The addition of cranberries helps reduce water weight—a little aesthetically pleasing benefit that makes you look good too.

Makes 1 serving
Prep Time: 5 minutes

3 tablespoons Truvani vanilla protein powder

2-inch piece fresh ginger root, peeled

2 cups dark leafy greens (kale, collards, romaine, spinach, chard, etc.)

1 cup chopped celery

1 cup mixed frozen berries of your choice (strawberries, blueberries, cranberries, etc.)

½ cup filtered water

Blend all the ingredients in a blender, stopping occasionally to scrape down the sides; or use a tamper/plunger to help blend the ingredients together. Thin with more water as needed to achieve a smooth consistency.

Serve immediately, or store in an airtight container for up to 1 day.

HARI SHAKE

Hari, my last name, means "green" in Hindi—so it just seemed like the right way to describe this everyday green smoothie. These green beauties make the perfect breakfast, late-afternoon snack, or even an appetizer at lunch or dinner! Use airtight glass containers to store your shakes.

Makes 1 serving
Prep Time: 10 minutes

2 cups kale
2 celery stalks, chopped
3 sprigs parsley
3 sprigs cilantro
1 pear, chopped
1 cup strawberries
Juice of ½ lemon
1 cup filtered water

Wash all ingredients and place them into a blender and blend to combine.

BLUEBERRY AVOCADO DELIGHT SMOOTHIE

Avocados are magical in smoothies. They add creaminess and healthy fat, which helps your body absorb all the nutrients in those antioxidant-rich blueberries!

Makes 1 serving
Prep Time: 5 minutes

1 cup frozen blueberries

1 cup loosely packed baby spinach

½ cup or more almond milk or coconut milk

½ ripe avocado, peeled and pitted

¼ cup filtered water, or more as needed

1 tablespoon chia seeds

1 to 2 teaspoons raw honey

Place all the ingredients in a blender and blend to combine, stopping occasionally to scrape down the sides; or use a tamper/plunger to help blend the ingredients together. Thin with more milk or water as needed.

POWER-UP PROTEIN SHAKE

An icy, chocolatey shake whipped up to taste like a frozen peanut butter cup? Yes, please! You'd never guess this yummy shake is healthy and packed with protein.

Makes 1 serving
Prep Time: 5 minutes

1 frozen ripe banana, cut into 4 pieces

3 tablespoons Truvani chocolate protein powder

2 tablespoons peanut butter

¾ cup liquid of choice (nut milk, coconut milk, filtered water, etc.)

Ice, as needed

Place all the ingredients in a blender and blend to combine, stopping occasionally to scrape down the sides as necessary; or use a tamper/plunger to help blend the ingredients together.

CABBAGE PATCH KID JUICE

The sweet taste of pear and cabbage in this juice will take you back to the good old days! Cabbage juice is absolutely amazing for your health. Making this juice, and juicing in general, is the best health insurance life can offer, period.

Makes 2 servings
Prep Time: 10 minutes

½ bunch collard leaves
½ head green cabbage
¼ bunch parsley
1 pear
2-inch piece fresh ginger root
1 cucumber, ends removed
1 lemon, peel removed

Wash all the ingredients thoroughly and juice in this order: collard leaves, cabbage, parsley, pear, ginger, cucumber, and lemon.

Stir the mixture before serving, and clean your juicer immediately.

RAVISHING RED JUICE

Definition of *ravishing*: unusually attractive, pleasing, or striking. I couldn't think of a better word to describe this juice. It's very attractive in color, pleasing to the eye, and striking to your system. This is a perfect juice for the morning—the beets do some serious cleansing work to help your body fight off a myriad of ailments.

Makes 2 servings
Prep Time: 10 minutes

½ bunch kale (optional)
¼ bunch parsley (optional)
5 carrots
1 beet, stems removed
½ bunch celery
1 green apple, cored
2-inch piece fresh ginger root
1 cucumber, ends removed

Wash all the ingredients thoroughly and juice in this order: kale, if using, then parsley, if using, then carrots, beet, celery, apple, ginger, and cucumber.

Stir the mixture before serving, and clean your juicer immediately.

CARIBBEAN SMOOTHIE

My friend made this smoothie for us on vacation using the only produce he could find on the island and it was one of the best smoothies I have ever had. I couldn't believe how incredible it turned out. The next morning, I made sure to wake up early so I could help him make it and steal the recipe! Haha!

Makes 1 serving
Prep Time: 10 minutes

2 cups loosely packed spinach leaves
2 carrots, peeled and chopped
½ cucumber, chopped
½ cup quartered strawberries
½ apple, unpeeled, cored and diced
½ orange, peeled
½ lime, juiced
Ice, as needed
1 cup filtered water

Place all the ingredients in a blender and blend to combine, stopping occasionally to scrape down the sides; or use a tamper/plunger to help blend the ingredients together.

HOMEMADE NUT MILK
3 WAYS

Here are three ways to make nut milk at home without all the nasty additives found in store-bought versions. The only supplies you'll need are a high-powered blender and a nut-milk bag—unless you make the cashew milk, as you don't even need to strain that one! Each batch will last about 3 days in the fridge.

ALMOND MILK

Makes 4 cups
Prep Time: 5 minutes, plus soaking time

1 cup almonds

4 cups filtered water, plus more for soaking

Place the almonds in a bowl of filtered water and let soak for at least 8 hours or overnight.

Rinse the almonds and place in a blender with 4 cups filtered water. Blend until well combined.

Strain using a nut-milk bag; can be stored in the refrigerator for up to 3 days.

CASHEW MILK

Makes 4 cups
Prep Time: 5 minutes, plus soaking time

1 cup cashews

4 cups filtered water, plus more for soaking

Place the cashews in a bowl of filtered water and let soak for at least 8 hours or overnight.

Rinse the cashews and place in a blender with 4 cups filtered water. Blend until well combined.

Store in the refrigerator for up to 3 days.

PISTACHIO MILK

Makes 4 cups
Prep Time: 5 minutes

1 cup pistachios

4 cups filtered water

Place the pistachios and water in a blender and blend to combine.

Strain using a nut-milk bag; can be stored in the refrigerator for up to 3 days.

How to Make Organic Coffee Anywhere:
Two-Minute Travel Hack

When I'm traveling, even if I'm staying someplace where there is a coffee shop on every corner, the last thing I want to do is buy a cup of coffee that isn't organic. That's because conventional coffee is typically imported and grown with large amounts of synthetic pesticides and insecticides. Not only do I want to avoid sipping on those in the morning, but organic fair-trade coffee tastes better too! The same caution goes to what the hotel provides in your room or via room service, and I wouldn't touch the little packets of dried nondairy creamers in my hotel room with a 10-foot pole. These are made with ingredients like corn syrup solids, heart-wrecking trans fats, artificial flavors, and emulsifiers. Bleh!

It doesn't have to be this way. With a few simple supplies, you could be sipping on delicious organic coffee anywhere on the planet! Whether you enjoy traveling or would just like to drink organic coffee while you're at the office, let me show you how I make coffee when I'm on the road.

Supplies you'll need to bring with you:

- **Stainless Steel Electric Kettle** Not only will this make hot water for your coffee, but you can use it to make tea and oatmeal too! This is well worth the investment and will pay for itself over and over again.

- **Organic Coconut Milk Powder** An organic coconut milk powder can be found online and in the baking section of many grocery stores. Look for one with a simple ingredient list and not packed with unnecessary additives.

- **Organic Freeze-Dried Instant Coffee** Instant coffee is not the type of coffee that I'd regularly drink at home, as I prefer to brew fresh coffee from organic coffee beans. But an instant version is a mess-free option that is perfect for when you are in a hotel room or somewhere else that you can't easily brew a pot of coffee. It also tastes surprisingly good and has just one ingredient: organic coffee! You can find it online and in many natural-foods stores.

FOOD BABE'S ORGANIC COFFEE ON-THE-GO

Makes 1 serving
Prep Time: 2 minutes

1 teaspoon organic instant coffee
1 teaspoon coconut milk powder
8 ounces hot filtered water

Place the instant coffee and powdered coconut milk in a coffee mug.

Pour the filtered hot water over the top and stir.

Tip: Add more coffee if you like a stronger cup, or add more coconut milk powder if you like it creamier. Have fun experimenting to find the perfect combination for your own preferences.

chapter 5

SOUPS AND SALADS

There's nothing like a light meal packed with veggies.
I have either a big salad or soup for lunch on most days, depending
on my mood. They're filling and don't leave me in a food coma.

MEXICAN LENTIL TORTILLA SOUP

Utilizing satisfying ingredients such as lentils that are packed with fiber and protein is a great way to lose excess pounds. I love to make a huge pot of this lentil soup at the beginning of the week—it's so simple. The pot lasts me for a few days and makes the perfect lunch reheated and topped off with half an avocado.

Makes 4 servings
Prep Time: 10 minutes
Cook Time: 35 minutes

2 tablespoons extra-virgin olive oil
½ yellow onion, diced
2 celery stalks, diced
3 carrots, diced
2 garlic cloves, minced
½ cup lentils, rinsed
6 cups vegetable broth
One 14-ounce jar crushed tomatoes
½ jalapeño pepper, seeded and minced
½ teaspoon ground cumin
½ teaspoon ground coriander
½ teaspoon sea salt
¼ teaspoon ground black pepper
¼ cup chopped fresh cilantro
3 sprouted corn tortillas, cut into ½-inch-wide pieces

Optional Toppings

1 sliced avocado
¼ cup crumbled goat cheese
1 lime

Heat the olive oil in a large pot over medium heat. Add the onion, celery, and carrots and cook until tender, 8 to 10 minutes.

Add the remaining ingredients. Bring to a boil, then turn down the heat to a simmer. Cook for 20 to 25 minutes.

Serve the soup topped with sliced avocado, goat cheese, and fresh lime, if desired.

SLIMMING TURKEY KALE SOUP

This particular soup recipe was in heavy rotation at my house right after Harley was born. With a new baby to care for, I needed something that was mindlessly easy to make, and it really helped me shed the extra baby weight. You also probably already have most of these ingredients in your kitchen right now, making it even easier to put together on a busy weeknight!

Makes 4 servings
Prep Time: 10 minutes
Cook Time: 30 Minutes

1 tablespoon olive oil
1 pound ground turkey breast
2 garlic cloves, minced
3 celery stalks, diced
2 carrots, diced
1 yellow onion, diced
1 teaspoon red pepper flakes
1 tablespoon dried Italian seasoning
2 teaspoons sea salt
½ teaspoon ground black pepper
2 cups chicken broth
2 cups filtered water
1 bay leaf
2 cups chopped kale

Heat the oil in a large pot over medium heat. Add the turkey and cook 3 to 4 minutes, or until slightly browned.

Add the garlic, celery, carrots, onion, red pepper, Italian seasoning, and salt and pepper. Cook for 5 minutes, or until vegetables are tender.

Add the chicken broth, 2 cups filtered water, and 1 bay leaf. Bring to a boil, then the reduce heat. Simmer the soup for 15 minutes. Remove the bay leaf and add the kale, simmering the soup for 5 additional minutes before serving.

CREAMY THAI CURRIED CARROT SOUP

This sweet-and-spicy vegan soup is just perfect to make on a rainy day. The spices really hit the spot and warm you right up. Serve it with a big green salad topped with lentils for extra protein.

Makes 4 servings
Prep Time: 15 minutes
Cook Time: 30 minutes

2 teaspoons coconut oil

1 yellow onion, diced

2 garlic cloves, chopped

1 pound carrots, peeled and sliced

2 cups vegetable broth, or more as needed

1¾ cups coconut milk (from one 13.5-ounce can)

2 tablespoons red curry paste

1 bay leaf

¼ teaspoon dried thyme

⅛ teaspoon ground nutmeg

Sea salt and ground black pepper to taste

¼ cup pumpkin seeds

¼ cup chopped cilantro

Heat the coconut oil in a large pot over medium heat. Add the onion, garlic, and carrots and sauté for 5 to 7 minutes.

Add the broth, coconut milk, curry paste, bay leaf, and thyme and cook over medium heat, stirring occasionally, until the carrots are tender, about 20 to 22 minutes.

Take off the heat, remove the bay leaf, and puree the mixture with an immersion blender or counter blender.

Place back on the stove and add more broth as needed to thin to desired consistency. Mix in the nutmeg and season with salt and pepper to taste. Heat until warmed through.

Top the soup with pumpkin seeds and chopped cilantro and serve.

MAGICAL MISO SOUP

Honestly, I didn't know about miso for most of my life. I had heard of miso soup and tried it at various sushi restaurants, but never really knew what it was or if it was good for me. As soon as I did some investigating into my own health, I quickly realized that fermented foods such as miso were absolutely crucial for a healthy diet. Miso paste is created from a mixture of soybeans, sea salt, and rice koji and then fermented. The fermentation process creates enzyme-rich compounds that are effective at detoxifying your body. Miso is very powerful!

Makes 4 servings
Prep Time: 5 minutes
Cook Time: 10 minutes

8 cups filtered water

1 sheet or ¼ cup nori, cut into large rectangles

½ cup chopped mushrooms or tofu

½ cup red or white miso paste

¾ cup chopped green onions

Sea salt to taste

Place the 8 cups of water in a large pot and bring to a low simmer.

Add the nori and mushrooms and simmer for 5 to 7 minutes.

Place the miso paste in a small bowl and add a little hot water. Whisk until smooth. Add the miso to the soup along with the green onions and stir well to combine. Simmer the soup for 3 minutes and serve immediately.

LENTIL DETOX SALAD

After coming home from vacation or eating heavy meals for a while, I like to make a big batch of this salad to reset my body. I call it a "detox" salad because it contains cilantro, which is a very detoxifying herb. There's actually no lettuce in this salad—the cilantro makes up all the greens. It's an herb I like to incorporate in juices and in soups, but especially in salads like this one. If you prefer, try arugula, parsley, or kale instead of cilantro. These leafy greens are healthy and help to detox the body too! You can enjoy the salad warm or make it ahead of time and store it in the fridge for a few days. Just wait until right before serving to dice and add the avocado so it won't turn brown.

Makes 4 servings
Prep Time: 5 minutes

2 red peppers, diced
1½ cups cooked lentils
2 cups chopped cilantro
2 tablespoons raisins or dried currants
1 avocado, peeled and diced

Place the salad ingredients in a bowl and set aside.

To make the vinaigrette, place all the ingredients in a separate bowl and whisk to combine.

Pour the vinaigrette over the salad and toss to combine. Serve immediately or store in the fridge up to 3 days.

CURRY VINAIGRETTE

2 tablespoons extra-virgin olive oil
¼ teaspoon sea salt
⅛ teaspoon ground black pepper
2 teaspoons curry powder
2 teaspoons raw honey
Juice of 1 lime

CHICKEN SHAWARMA SALAD

The flavors in this salad are out of this world. It's made with a handful of common spices you probably already have in your pantry. But don't let the simplicity fool you! Give it a try. I think you'll be pleasantly surprised. You can make it vegetarian by substituting chickpeas for the chicken—this salad is delicious either way.

Makes 2 servings
Prep Time: 30 minutes
Cook Time: 10 to 15 minutes

2 skinless boneless chicken breasts (to make it vegetarian, use 1½ cups cooked chickpeas)

2 tablespoons olive oil

Juice of ½ lemon

½ teaspoon ground coriander

½ teaspoon ground cumin

½ teaspoon ground paprika

¼ teaspoon ground turmeric

⅛ teaspoon ground cinnamon

Pinch of sea salt and ground black pepper

1 celery stalk, diced

½ small red onion, diced

¼ cup avocado oil mayonnaise

2 tablespoons chopped Italian parsley

Baby romaine or butter lettuce leaves or mixed greens

Place the chicken breasts in a glass container and add the oil, lemon juice, and spices. Let the chicken marinate for ½ hour or cover and refrigerate overnight.

Heat a sauté pan over medium heat and add the chicken. Cook 2 minutes per side, then cover, reduce heat to medium-low, and cook until no longer pink inside, turning once, about 10 minutes. Dice and place in a bowl.

Add the celery, onion, mayonnaise, and parsley to the chicken. Mix well to combine. Serve with lettuce leaves as wraps or on top of a bed of greens.

Tip: If making the vegetarian option, mix the chickpeas with the oil, lemon juice, and spices, and let the mixture sit for 15 minutes. Mash the chickpeas slightly before combining with the celery, onion, parsley, and mayonnaise.

JEWELED KALE SALAD

Combining sweet juicy ingredients such as pomegranate seeds with dark leafy greens is a real winner. This salad is one of my in-laws' favorites and I make it for them during the holidays. SCORE!

Makes 4 servings
Prep Time: 10 minutes

5 cups curly kale, chopped

Juice of 1 lemon

2 tablespoons extra-virgin olive oil

2 teaspoons raw honey

Sea salt and ground black pepper to taste

½ cup pomegranate seeds

½ cup toasted pine nuts

Process the kale into small pieces in a food processor.

To make the dressing, stir the lemon juice, olive oil, honey, salt, and pepper together in a large bowl.

Add the kale, pomegranate seeds, and pine nuts to the bowl with the dressing. Toss all the ingredients together and serve.

SWEET CRUNCH SALAD

This salad contains two underappreciated ingredients that I believe people should eat more of: radicchio and Brazil nuts! Radicchio is packed with antioxidants and vitamin K—which is great for your heart and can help fight cancer. Brazil nuts are among the top sources of selenium, a nutrient that is good for the health of your heart and thyroid, and is a powerful antioxidant. Many people don't get enough selenium, but you only need to eat 1 or 2 Brazil nuts to get your daily dose. So dig in and give it a try!

Makes 4 servings
Prep Time: 15 minutes

1 large head radicchio, finely chopped
1 red apple, julienned
¼ cup currants
6 Brazil nuts, chopped
2 scallions, chopped

Place all the salad ingredients in a bowl and toss to combine.

To make the dressing, whisk together all the ingredients. Pour over the salad and toss.

DRESSING

¼ cup extra-virgin olive oil
2 tablespoons champagne vinegar
1 teaspoon Dijon mustard
1 teaspoon raw honey
Sea salt and ground black pepper to taste

GRAPEFRUIT GODDESS SALAD

This tart, sweet, crunchy, and juicy salad is such a nice departure from typical salad ingredients. The combo bursts with flavor and has an amazing ability to zap sugar cravings.

Makes 4 servings
Prep Time: 10 minutes

4 cups baby arugula
1 fennel bulb, thinly sliced
1 avocado, peeled and sliced
1 grapefruit, peeled and segmented
¼ small red onion, thinly sliced
¼ cup toasted pine nuts or walnuts
2 tablespoons chopped fresh dill

VINAIGRETTE

3 tablespoons grapefruit juice
3 tablespoons extra-virgin olive oil
1 tablespoon apple cider vinegar
1 teaspoon Dijon mustard
Sea salt and ground black pepper
to taste

Place all the salad ingredients in a bowl and toss to combine.

To make the vinaigrette, whisk all the ingredients together. Pour over the salad and serve.

SUPERFOOD SPROUT SALAD

This sprout salad is so good, so refreshing, and so healthy! It's perfect to make ahead the night before for lunch-to-go. It also makes a great side dish for dinner. I've even eaten it for breakfast. Yes, I know I can be a little intense about getting my vegetables in.

Makes 4 servings
Prep Time: 10 minutes

8 large carrots, shredded
1 cup blueberries
Zest and juice of 1 lemon
4 tablespoons nut butter
2 cups finely chopped spinach
2 cups sprouts
½ cup sunflower seeds
Sea salt and ground black pepper to taste

Combine the carrots, blueberries, lemon zest, lemon juice, and nut butter in a large bowl and toss to combine.

Add the spinach, sprouts, sunflower seeds, salt, and pepper and mix together. Serve.

chapter 6

SNACKS AND FUN FOOD

Who doesn't love to eat chips and dip? I figured out how to make my favorite "junk foods" in healthy ways and now I have accumulated a bunch of fun food recipes for parties, outdoor cookouts, and movie nights at home. Keep these handy for the next time you've got company or just want something fun to eat yourself.

CREAMY KALE ARTICHOKE DIP

This is one of my favorite appetizers to make for any get together, to take to a party, or just to have while watching something really great on TV. This dip is full of vegetables and the nutmeg and cayenne pepper really take the flavor up a notch. If you know someone who is wary of kale (maybe it's you), this recipe will be a revelation. It's rich, creamy, and delicious.

Makes 8 servings
Prep Time: 5 minutes
Cook Time: 45 minutes

1 bag frozen artichoke hearts, thawed and chopped

4 cups finely chopped kale

1 garlic clove, minced

1 cup sour cream

3 tablespoons mayonnaise

3 tablespoons raw Parmesan, plus more to top

1 tablespoon coconut oil

1 teaspoon sea salt

1 teaspoon ground black pepper

⅛ teaspoon ground nutmeg

⅛ teaspoon cayenne pepper

Preheat the oven to 375°F. Grease an 8 x 8-inch baking dish with coconut oil.

Place all the ingredients in a large bowl and mix well to combine.

Pour the mixture into the greased baking dish and top with additional Parmesan cheese, if desired. Cover and bake for 30 to 45 minutes.

Remove the dip from the oven and let sit for at least 5 minutes before serving.

CHEESY CHIPS (HOMEMADE DORITOS!)

My husband created these because he is addicted to chips. I was so excited to see him making his own cheesy tortilla chips in the kitchen because these are *so much better* for you than those popular bagged "nacho cheese" chips in stores that are fried in unhealthy oils and covered in dyes and MSG—bleh!

Makes 4 servings
Prep Time: 10 minutes
Cook Time: 16 minutes

2 tablespoons grated Romano cheese
1½ teaspoons chili powder
½ teaspoon paprika
½ teaspoon garlic powder
½ teaspoon buttermilk powder
¼ teaspoon onion powder
¼ teaspoon sea salt
8 corn tortillas
(recipe page 171)
Olive oil spray

Preheat the oven to 350°F.

Mix the first 7 ingredients together and set aside.

Stack the tortillas; cut them in half, then cut each half into thirds, forming triangle-shaped pieces. Place half of the tortilla triangles in a single layer on a rack set over a baking sheet. Spray the top of each tortilla with olive oil and sprinkle with half of the seasoning mix.

Bake for 8 minutes on each side or until almost crisp. The chips will finish crisping as they cool. Repeat with the remaining tortilla triangles.

WRAPPED BRIE

We love to enjoy this Brie at home as a little treat in the kitchen while cooking up a big dinner on the weekend for friends. This super simple dish is easy to prepare, especially when you use store-bought puff pastry dough. Just make sure you don't use a processed pastry dough by a company with "Farm" in the name who makes theirs with hydrogenated cottonseed oil and high-fructose corn syrup. Serve it with some crackers, celery, and apple slices. Fun dinners with this appetizer are the best.

Makes 4 to 6 servings
Prep Time: 10 minutes
Cook Time: 30 minutes

One 14-ounce puff pastry dough, thawed
12 ounces grass-fed Brie
½ cup fruit preserve of choice
1 egg, beaten

Preheat the oven to 425°F.

Unfold the thawed pastry dough and lay flat on a parchment-lined baking sheet. Place the Brie in the middle of the thawed dough.

Add the fruit preserves atop the Brie and wrap with the pastry dough, pinching in the edges to seal.

Brush the dough-wrapped Brie with the beaten egg and bake for 10 minutes. Reduce the heat to 350°F and bake for an additional 20 minutes.

Let cool for at least 10 minutes before serving.

HEALING TURMERIC HUMMUS

I've been making my own hummus for many years. I don't buy the premade stuff for lots of reasons, namely because most brands are made with inflammatory soybean oil or canola oil and simply don't taste anywhere near as good as fresh homemade hummus. Hummus has a combo of protein and fiber to keep you from craving junk. I love to snack on it with red bell pepper, carrots, or celery sticks almost every day. It's too easy not to try!

Makes 2 to 4 servings
Prep Time: 10 minutes

1½ cups cooked or one 15.5-ounce can chickpeas, rinsed and drained

2 tablespoons tahini

1 garlic clove, minced

2 tablespoons chopped parsley

Juice of ½ lemon

½ teaspoon ground turmeric

¼ teaspoon ground cumin

¼ teaspoon ground paprika

¼ teaspoon sea salt

¼ teaspoon ground black pepper

2 tablespoons extra-virgin olive oil

Crudités

Combine the first 10 ingredients in a food processor, scraping the sides as needed.

With the food processor running, slowly add the oil until well combined.

Serve with fresh chopped vegetables or other desired accompaniments. The hummus keeps at least 5 days in the fridge.

THE BEST-EVER CHICKEN WINGS

My husband LOVES chicken wings—it's one of his top three favorite foods, next to pizza and steak. He enjoys grilling pasture-raised wings with a little sea salt, pepper, and coconut oil—really simple and they turn out pretty good—but this recipe with Indian spices takes them to a whole other level. We use organic grass-fed yogurt in the marinade, which makes the chicken extra juicy and tender. When they come off the grill, they are crispy, light, so flavorful, and waaaaaay better for you than anything you can get out in a restaurant.

Makes 12 wings
Prep Time: 60 minutes
Cook Time: 30 minutes

1 pound organic raw chicken wings
1 cup plain yogurt
1 lemon, juiced
1 teaspoon sea salt
½ teaspoon ground black pepper
½ teaspoon ground cumin
½ teaspoon ground paprika
½ teaspoon ground coriander
¼ teaspoon ground cardamom
¼ teaspoon ground ginger
¼ teaspoon cayenne pepper
¼ teaspoon ground turmeric
¼ cup chopped cilantro

Preheat a grill or preheat the oven to 425°F.

Combine all the ingredients, except the cilantro, in a bowl and marinate for at least 1 hour.

Cook the wings on the grill, turning occasionally, for about 25 to 30 minutes or until cooked through. You can also bake the wings on a wire rack in the oven for about 45 minutes.

Serve immediately, sprinkled with chopped cilantro.

BUFFALO CAULIFLOWER BITES

These make a great alternative to buffalo chicken wings, and I think you'll be surprised at how hearty and delicious cauliflower can taste. Unlike buffalo wings that are almost always from factory-farmed chicken and packed with artificial ingredients, these are actually HEALTHY and packed with fiber and nutrients! Eat a few of these and you'll instantly zap away cravings for processed junk food filled with MSG and added sugar.

Makes 4 to 6 servings
Prep Time: 10 minutes
Cook Time: 20 minutes

½ cup spelt flour
½ cup plus 2 tablespoons almond milk
1 teaspoon hot sauce
½ teaspoon garlic powder
Pinch of sea salt and ground black pepper
1 head cauliflower, chopped into florets

Preheat the oven to 425°F.

Place the flour, milk, hot sauce, garlic, and salt and pepper in a bowl. Whisk to combine.

Dredge the cauliflower florets in the flour mix until well coated. Using a slotted spoon, remove the cauliflower and place on a greased rimmed baking sheet. Bake until pale golden brown, about 15 minutes.

While the cauliflower is baking, make the buffalo sauce. Place all the ingredients in a bowl and whisk to combine.

Pour the hot sauce evenly over the cauliflower florets while they're still on the baking sheet. Toss to combine and place back in the oven for 5 minutes.

If making the yogurt dill sauce, place all the ingredients in a bowl and mix to combine.

To serve, place the cauliflower bites on a plate and top with yogurt dill sauce and optional toppings such as chopped carrot, celery, and parsley.

BUFFALO SAUCE

½ cup hot sauce
¼ cup distilled white vinegar or apple cider vinegar
1 teaspoon prepared horseradish
¼ teaspoon ground paprika

YOGURT DILL SAUCE

½ cup plain yogurt
1 tablespoon fresh dill
1 teaspoon lemon juice
Pinch of sea salt and ground black pepper

Optional Toppings

1 carrot, diced
1 celery stalk, diced
2 tablespoons chopped parsley

EASY BROCCOLI BITES

What a fun way to eat broccoli! Kids love these and picky adults do too. These little puppies are packed with healthy veggies but are so fun to eat that they'll barely notice. Dip them in organic ketchup or eat them plain.

Makes 4 Servings or 12 broccoli bites
Prep Time: 15 minutes
Cook Time: 20 minutes

1 cup cooked millet or quinoa
½ cup diced broccoli florets
¼ cup cooked white beans
¼ cup diced carrots
¼ cup diced yellow onion
1 garlic clove, peeled
2 tablespoons coconut oil
2 teaspoons ground flaxseed
1 teaspoon apple cider vinegar
1 teaspoon sea salt
½ teaspoon dried basil
½ teaspoon dried oregano
Olive oil for greasing

Preheat the oven to 400°F.

Place all the ingredients in a food processor and pulse until a rough paste forms. You will need to stop and scrape down the sides a couple of times.

Let the mixture sit for 10 minutes.

Using a small scooper, place balls of the mixture on a parchment-lined baking sheet, flattening each ball slightly with the underside of the scoop. Spray the top of each with olive oil and bake until golden, about 10 minutes per side.

THE BEST GUACAMOLE

Yep, I snuck some spinach in there! I know it's not conventional to add greens to guacamole, but I like to pump up the nutritional value. You can add any type of greens that you like. The key is to chop them up very finely so that they blend in with the rest of the ingredients.

Makes 4 servings
Prep Time: 10 minutes

2 avocados, peeled and mashed
6 cilantro sprigs, finely chopped
1 cup spinach, finely chopped
1 tomato, chopped
¼ red onion, diced
1 jalapeno, seeded and diced
1 garlic clove, minced
1 lime, juiced
¼ teaspoon of sea salt

Place all the ingredients in a small bowl and mix well to combine.

Serve with veggie sticks or homemade tortilla chips.

ROASTED HEIRLOOM TOMATO SALSA

This salsa is the BEST with heirloom tomatoes from the farmers market. Homemade salsa is a must for serving with any Mexican dish, and this is my go-to recipe. For a milder salsa, remove the pith and seeds from the chiles before roasting—or leave them in for a spicier taste!

Makes 6 to 8 servings
Prep Time: 10 minutes
Cook Time: 25 minutes

1 jalapeño pepper, stemmed and cut lengthwise into 4 strips

1 serrano pepper, stemmed and cut lengthwise in ½

1 poblano pepper, stemmed and cut lengthwise into 6 strips

½ yellow onion, chopped

2 garlic cloves, peeled

3 heirloom tomatoes, cut in quarters

1 cup canned fire-roasted tomatoes

¼ cup chopped fresh cilantro

1 teaspoon sea salt

½ teaspoon ground black pepper

Preheat the oven to 400°F.

Place the peppers, onion, garlic, and heirloom tomatoes on a rimmed baking sheet and bake until lightly roasted, about 25 minutes.

Transfer the roasted vegetables to a food processor. Add the canned tomatoes, cilantro, and salt and pepper and pulse to your desired consistency. Refrigerate the salsa until ready to serve.

SWEET POTATO SKINS

If you need a healthy appetizer to serve instead of the usual chips and salsa or fried mozzarella sticks, these will knock your socks off! They also look beautiful on a platter for a big party or game night. These babies have a sweet-and-salty thing going that makes them irresistible; I even eat them for lunch sometimes. They really hit the spot!

Makes 8 to 10 servings
Prep Time: 10 minutes
Cook Time: 35 minutes

8 small sweet potatoes
2 tablespoons coconut oil
3 avocados, peeled and pitted
1 large tomato, diced
¼ cup diced red onion
½ jalapeño, diced
1 lime, juiced
¼ cup chopped cilantro
Sea salt and ground black pepper to taste
1 cup cooked black beans
1 cup shredded cheddar cheese

Preheat the oven to 400°F.

Rub each sweet potato with coconut oil and place on a sheet pan in the oven for 25 to 30 minutes or until they are fork tender.

While the sweet potatoes are cooking, make the guacamole. Start by mashing the avocado. Add the tomato, onion, jalapeño, lime juice, and cilantro. Season with salt and pepper to taste. Set aside.

When the sweet potatoes are done, cut each one in half and scoop out half the filling. Set the filling aside.

Layer the black beans on each sweet potato half and then layer the cheese on top of the beans. Place them back in the oven to melt the cheese, 3 to 4 minutes.

When the cheese is melted, take the skins out of the oven and top with a scoop of guacamole.

chapter 7

MAIN DISHES

I learned a long time ago that getting a healthy home-cooked meal on the table doesn't need to be difficult or time-consuming. That's why most of my recipes take less than 30 minutes to prepare with a handful of ingredients. Whether I'm making decadent salmon or an entire roasted chicken with vegetables, I'm so happy knowing that it can be done almost any night of the week. Mission accomplished!

WHITE BEAN CHILI

This white bean chili is a favorite around here. Sometimes I add in ground turkey, sometimes I don't—it's totally adaptable to any dietary preferences, and it turns out delicious every single time. The best part is that it satisfies any craving for chili, so you don't need to turn to those canned versions spiked with MSG and other synthetic flavor enhancers. If you want to always have some handy, freeze this chili in individual jars that you can defrost and heat up when the time is right.

Makes 4 to 6 servings
Prep Time: 10 minutes
Cook Time: 45 minutes

1 tablespoon olive oil
2 green bell peppers, chopped
1 large onion, chopped
4 cups vegetable broth
3 cups cooked cannellini beans
One 16-ounce jar tomatillo salsa
One 4-ounce can diced green chiles, drained
1 small jalapeño, seeded and finely sliced
2 tablespoons ground cumin
1 teaspoon ground coriander
1 teaspoon dried oregano
½ teaspoon sea salt
1 bay leaf
1 cup chopped fresh cilantro
1 lime, cut into wedges

Heat the oil in a large pot over medium-high heat.

Add the bell pepper and onion and cook until softened, 3 to 4 minutes.

Add the remaining ingredients, except the cilantro and lime. Reduce the heat and simmer for 35 to 40 minutes.

Take off the heat, stir in the cilantro, and serve with a lime wedge.

QUINOA VEGGIE BURGERS
with Beet Root French Fries

I'm always concocting new veggie burger recipes at home, now that I no longer buy packaged or processed veggie burgers because of the scary ingredients and additives they contain. These quinoa veggie burgers are FABULOUS and too EASY *not* to make ASAP. You can make several ahead of time and either freeze or refrigerate them to enjoy later. They also make a perfect burger to bring to a cookout. Just have the grill master plop them on the grill to reheat and you've got a delicious plant-based, protein-packed meal.

Makes 4 servings
Prep Time: 30 minutes
Cook Time: 30 minutes

1 cup cooked quinoa, room temperature
1 baked sweet potato, skin removed, mashed, room temperature
1 egg or 1 tablespoon ground flaxseed mixed with 3 tablespoons filtered water
¼ cup chopped fresh cilantro
½ small yellow onion, diced
1-inch piece fresh ginger root, minced
1 garlic clove, minced
½ teaspoon sea salt
½ teaspoon garam masala
½ teaspoon curry powder
¼ teaspoon ground mustard seed (optional)
⅛ teaspoon cayenne pepper
Melted coconut oil for brushing burgers

BEET ROOT FRENCH FRIES

2 large beets, washed, peeled, and cut into long rectangular strips
1 tablespoon coconut oil, melted
¼ teaspoon sea salt

Preheat the oven to 400°F.

Combine all the ingredients for the burgers, except the coconut oil, in a large bowl. Form into 8 patties using a generous ¼ cup of mixture for each.

Line a baking sheet with parchment and brush with coconut oil. Place the patties on the oiled parchment and brush with a small amount of coconut oil. Bake for 15 minutes, or until the bottoms brown. Using a metal spatula, flip the patties over and bake 5 to 10 minutes longer.

To make the Beet Root French Fries: Toss the beet strips with oil and sprinkle with sea salt.

Place the beets in a single layer on a parchment-lined baking sheet and bake until tender, about 30 minutes, rotating halfway through. Serve immediately.

MEXICAN PIZZA

Have you ever tried to eat healthfully at a Mexican restaurant? It's not an easy endeavor! That's because practically everything is fried and made with refined vegetable oils. But let's face it, going out to a Mexican restaurant and avoiding the chips, tortillas, enchiladas, etc. is *not fun!* So instead of putting myself in that situation, I make this amazing meal at home; it's easy and satisfies my Mexican food cravings like no other. If you like Mexican food as much as I do, you will love it too. This recipe is technically a tostada—but I like calling it pizza!

Makes 3 servings
Prep Time: 10 minutes
Cook Time: 15 minutes

6 corn tortillas
1½ cups salsa
1 tablespoon chili powder
2 cups cooked black beans
1 green pepper, chopped
½ yellow onion, chopped
½ jalapeño pepper, thinly sliced
1 cup cheddar cheese
2 cups romaine lettuce
1 lime, sliced
1 avocado, sliced

Preheat the oven to 400°F.

As the oven is preheating, place the corn tortillas on a rack in the oven for 3 to 4 minutes.

Remove the corn tortillas and top each with ¼ cup salsa, a pinch of chili powder, and equal portions of the black beans, green peppers, onions, jalapeño, and cheese.

Place the assembled tortillas back in the oven and bake for 8 to 10 minutes.

Serve with chopped romaine, a slice of lime, and avocado.

CORN TORTILLAS

The texture and freshness of these homemade corn tortillas can't be beat. They are so much better than tortillas that you buy in supermarkets. Once you try these, it will be hard to go back to any store-bought version ever again!

Makes 12 tortillas
Prep Time: 15 minutes
Cook Time: 12 minutes

2 cups masa harina whole corn flour
¾ teaspoon sea salt
1½ cups filtered water
2 tablespoons grass-fed butter

Mix flour and salt in a bowl. Add water and stir gently until the flour is mixed in (don't overmix).

Knead dough on a floured surface for 2 to 3 minutes.

Divide dough into 12 equal balls, and place them onto a plate.

Set a cast-iron griddle over medium heat, making sure that the surface is clean. Heat the butter.

Press a dough ball in your tortilla press and then carefully place the flat raw tortilla onto the griddle. Cook the first side for approximately 30 seconds, then flip and cook the second side for 30 seconds before removing to a plate, covering to keep warm. Continue to cook all remaining tortillas.

EGGPLANT PARM FROM THE FARM

This gorgeous (not fried) eggplant Parm was inspired by an Easter trip to Italy. Hands down, Italy has the tastiest food in the world. I always come home to my kitchen inspired after my travels there. For this recipe, instead of the mozzarella cheese that would traditionally be on top, I use raw unpasteurized goat's milk cheese and Parmesan. If it's available to you locally, I believe that raw unpasteurized cheese is the best choice. Raw dairy products are "alive" and have all of their probiotics, vitamins, and enzymes intact. If you don't have grass-fed or raw available to you, at least get a certified organic variety.

Makes 4 to 6 servings
Prep Time: 15 minutes
Cook Time: 75 minutes

1 cup quinoa, cooked
1 large eggplant
1 tablespoon olive oil
1 large yellow onion, chopped
3 garlic cloves, minced
8 ripe tomatoes, diced
½ teaspoon red pepper flakes
½ cup fresh basil, divided
½ teaspoon sea salt
3 ounces crumbled raw goat's milk cheese
2 ounces shredded raw Parmesan cheese

Preheat the oven to 400°F.

Cook the quinoa according to the package instructions.

Thinly slice the eggplant (½ inch thick) and place on a large baking rack sprayed with olive oil. Bake for 10 to 15 minutes, or until slightly golden brown.

Heat a sauté pan with oil over medium heat. Add the onions and garlic and cook for 4 to 5 minutes.

Add the tomatoes, red pepper flakes, ¼ cup basil, and salt and bring to a boil. Turn down the heat and simmer for 10 minutes.

To assemble, place ½ of the tomato sauce on the bottom of a 10 x 7-inch baking dish.

Layer the following ingredients 1 at a time: eggplant slices, quinoa, and remaining sauce. Top with cheese and remaining ¼ cup basil.

Bake covered at 350°F for 30 to 40 minutes.

STORMY DAY STIR-FRY

This is a recipe I discovered while working in Detroit. It's a staple at one of my favorite restaurants in the whole wide world—Inn Season Café. I loved this stir-fry so much that I ordered it every single time I went there and wanted to know what the secret was for making it so delicious. I was desperate, so what did I do? I called the chef one evening when I was craving this dish, and he was more than willing to share the ingredients with me and explain how easy it was to make. I was so shocked and ridiculously excited!

Makes 4 servings
Prep Time: 10 minutes
Cook Time: 40 minutes

2 teaspoons toasted sesame oil
¼ cup minced fresh ginger root
2 tablespoons low-sodium tamari
1 small head of cauliflower, broken into small florets
2 cups chopped red cabbage
1 small red onion, sliced
3 carrots, chopped
3 celery stalks, chopped
1 cup brown basmati rice, cooked according to package instructions
½ cup toasted cashews

Heat the sesame oil in a large wok over medium-high heat.

Add the ginger and sauté until it absorbs all the oil, about 2 minutes.

Add the tamari, 2 tablespoons filtered water, and the remaining vegetables.

Cook for up to 15 minutes, or until the vegetables are crisp-tender, periodically covering the wok to steam the vegetables and stirring as needed.

Serve the vegetables over basmati rice and topped with toasted cashews.

BETTER THAN TAKEOUT PAD THAI

I love eating pad thai, but (almost) every time I look to order it in a restaurant, MSG is already in the sauce which they can't omit. *Womp womp!* That's why I love to make my own. I also like to switch up my nut butters—sometimes I use almond butter instead of the usual peanut butter often found in pad thai recipes. Peanuts are more susceptible to being contaminated with aflatoxin, which is associated with an increased risk of liver cancer—so it's not a nut butter I eat on a daily basis. Besides, almond butter has a nutritional edge over peanut butter. I'm all for getting the most nutrition out of my meals!

Makes 4 servings
Prep Time: 15 minutes
Cook Time: 15 minutes

8-ounce package wide brown rice pad thai noodles
2 tablespoons coconut oil
2 cups broccoli florets
2 carrots, grated
½ yellow onion, thinly sliced
2 garlic cloves, minced
Sea salt and ground black pepper to taste
2 scallions, chopped
4 lime wedges

ALMOND SAUCE

2 tablespoons almond butter
½ cup low-sodium tamari
¼ cup apple cider vinegar
4 teaspoons raw honey
Large pinch of red pepper flakes

Cook the noodles according to the package instructions and set aside.

While the noodles are cooking, make the almond sauce: Mix the almond butter with ½ cup of hot water and whisk until combined. Add the tamari, vinegar, honey, and pepper flakes and whisk again until combined.

Heat the coconut oil in a large deep skillet over medium-high heat. Add the broccoli, carrots, and onion and cook for 4 to 5 minutes. Add the garlic and cook an additional 1 minute.

Add the rice noodles and almond sauce to the pan; toss to combine and heat through. Season with salt and pepper to taste. Take off the heat and top with scallions and lime wedges.

BAJA FISH TACOS
with Spicy Avocado Crème

Every night could be taco night at my house! Okay, maybe not every night, but fish tacos are among my all-time favorite foods. The spicy, fresh taste keeps me coming back to this recipe time and time again. I like to top mine with extra cilantro . . . and lime juice . . . and avocado crème—it's alllll so good.

Makes 8 tacos (4 servings)
Prep Time: 15 minutes
Cook Time: 20 minutes

1 teaspoon chili powder
½ teaspoon ground cumin
¼ teaspoon paprika
8 ounces wild-caught red snapper
Sea salt and ground black pepper
1 avocado, halved, pitted, peeled
1 garlic clove, peeled
½ lime, juiced
1 teaspoon hot sauce
Eight 6-inch sprouted corn tortillas
1 cup shredded red cabbage
¼ cup crumbled goat feta cheese
¼ cup chopped fresh cilantro
2 limes, cut into wedges

Preheat the oven to 375°F.

Mix together the chili powder, cumin, and paprika in a small bowl.

Line a baking sheet with parchment paper. Place the fish on the baking sheet and sprinkle with the seasoning mix. Season with salt and pepper. Bake for 18 to 20 minutes, or until flaky.

Place the avocado, garlic, lime juice, and hot sauce in a blender or food processor and blend well to combine, adding filtered water by tablespoons if the consistency is too thick.

Toast the tortillas 1 at a time over an open flame or in a skillet over high heat for about 30 seconds, or until warm and softened, turning frequently with tongs.

To serve, place some of the shredded cabbage on each tortilla. Top with the fish, goat cheese, cilantro, and a drizzle of avocado crème. Squeeze fresh lime juice on top.

MAKE-YOUR-OWN "CHICK-FIL-A" SANDWICH

I had an early love affair with Chick-fil-A. While in college, I'd eat there at least three to four times a week, sometimes more. I'd pick up a sandwich on my way back from the gym and thought it was healthy because it was around 400 calories. If only I knew then what I do now about their food. I'm a firm believer that if you love to eat something, you can find a way to make it at home without health-wrecking ingredients. That's when this sandwich was born. And, it tastes very close to the real thing. Pretty amazing, huh?

Makes 4 servings
Prep Time: 15 minutes
Cook Time: 40 minutes

2 skinless boneless chicken breasts

Sea salt and ground black pepper

1½ teaspoons paprika, divided

1 cup pickle juice

12 pickle slices

3 tablespoons apple cider vinegar

1 cup spelt flour

1 tablespoon powdered sugar

¼ teaspoon baking soda

¼ teaspoon dry mustard

1 large egg

½ cup unsweetened almond milk

Olive oil or coconut oil

4 sprouted whole wheat hamburger buns

1 tablespoon butter

Cut chicken breasts in half, making 4 similar-size pieces. Pound each chicken piece to ½-inch thick with a meat tenderizer or small hammer.

Place the chicken in a glass container and sprinkle with salt, pepper, and ½ teaspoon paprika. Add the pickle juice and let the chicken marinate for at least 4 hours or overnight.

Preheat the oven to 425°F.

Place the pickle slices in vinegar and let them marinate while you prep the chicken.

Combine the flour, sugar, baking soda, remaining teaspoon of paprika, and dry mustard in a bowl. Set aside.

Whisk together the egg and almond milk in a separate bowl.

Remove the chicken from the marinade. Dredge each piece in the egg bath, ensuring each side is wet, then dredge each in the flour mixture, coating each side completely. Place the chicken on a wire rack set over a baking sheet.

Sprinkle each chicken piece liberally with olive oil, covering both sides. Bake for 25 minutes, turning each piece halfway through.

Let the chicken rest for 5 minutes. While the chicken is resting, butter the hamburger buns and place in the oven for 3 to 5 minutes.

To assemble, place 3 pickles on each of 4 bun halves, add the chicken, and top with the remaining bun halves.

STUNNING STUFFED SQUASH

This dish not only looks beautiful served, but it will have your taste buds singing songs of downright deliciousness! Squash are so inexpensive (even organically grown!). Pick your favorite variety and start stuffing. Squash is also incredibly healthy: It's one of those more hearty vegetables that can replace grains in a meal and really fill you up. Best of all, there's little cleanup; you don't even have to use a plate if you don't want to—the bowl is natural and biodegradable.

Makes 4 servings
Prep Time: 20 minutes
Cook Time: 45 minutes

2 small delicata or acorn squash

4 tablespoons extra-virgin olive oil, divided

1 cup diced yellow onion

3 garlic cloves, minced

1 pound ground turkey or chicken

1 medium apple, diced

2 teaspoons dried sage

1 teaspoon fennel seeds

Sea salt and ground black pepper to taste

2 eggs, beaten

Preheat the oven to 400°F.

Place the squash on a cutting board and cut in half using a heavy large knife. Scoop out the seeds. Place the squash cut side up on a baking sheet and bake for 20 to 25 minutes, then set aside.

Heat 2 tablespoons oil in a large skillet over medium heat. Add the onion, garlic, and turkey and cook until no longer pink, 5 to 7 minutes. Add the diced apple, sage, and fennel and cook 4 to 5 minutes longer. Season with salt and pepper.

Take off the heat and stir in the eggs. Mound the stuffing into each of the squash halves and drizzle the remaining oil over the top. Bake for 30 to 35 minutes, or until the squash is fork tender.

FOOLPROOF ROASTED CHICKEN

There's this little restaurant in Paris that serves the most amazing roast chicken. The only problem? I don't live in Paris and the bird costs 75 euros! This whole roasted chicken reminds me of that dish, and you can make it using pastured-raised and/or organic chicken for much less money. It's the perfect chicken to roast before making bone broth or to eat off of all week long.

Makes 4 to 6 servings
Prep Time: 10 minutes
Cook Time: 90 minutes

1 whole chicken (3 to 4 pounds)
4 tablespoons butter
2 tablespoons olive oil
1½ teaspoons sea salt
½ teaspoon ground black pepper
½ lemon, juiced
3 fresh rosemary sprigs
½ lemon

Preheat the oven to 375°F.

Place the chicken in a roasting pan.

Mix together the butter, oil, salt, pepper, and lemon juice. Massage the mixture over the chicken.

Stuff the chicken with the rosemary and ½ lemon. Bake until an instant-read thermometer inserted into the thickest part of the thigh registers 165°F, about 1¼ to 1½ hours.

Spoon the fat off the pan juices, then add ½ cup filtered water to the pan. Set the pan over the stove top and bring to a boil, scraping up the browned bits. Pour the juices over the chicken to serve.

GRILLED PINEAPPLE TURKEY BURGERS

There's something so special about adding sliced grilled pineapple to burgers. The sweet-and-savory combination takes turkey burgers up a notch and really hits the spot.

Makes 4 servings (4 burgers)
Prep Time: 10 minutes
Cook Time: 10 minutes

1 pound ground turkey
¼ cup chopped yellow onion
1 tablespoon olive oil
1 teaspoon sea salt
¼ teaspoon ground black pepper
1 pineapple, peeled, cored, and cut into ½-inch rings
4 romaine lettuce leaves
4 burger buns
1 avocado, peeled and mashed

Preheat the grill to 400°F. (You can also use a cast-iron pan to cook the burgers and pineapple.)

Mix together the turkey, onion, oil, salt, and pepper. Form into four 4-inch round patties.

Place the patties on the grill and cook for 4 to 5 minutes per side, until cooked through. While the burgers are cooking, place the pineapple slices on the grill and cook until caramelized in spots, 2 to 3 minutes per side. Set aside when done.

To serve, place romaine lettuce on each burger bun and top with some of the mashed avocado. Place a turkey burger on top along with a pineapple slice.

TURKEY MEATBALL PASTA

These tasty meatballs are perfect with any kind of pasta—whole wheat, lentil, or even spaghetti squash! I've enjoyed them on their own and with a big salad too. They are so versatile.

Makes 4 servings
Prep Time: 15 minutes
Cook Time: 20 minutes

1 pound ground turkey

1 egg, beaten

1 teaspoon fennel seed

¼ teaspoon dried oregano

¼ teaspoon garlic powder

¼ teaspoon dried rosemary

¼ teaspoon dried thyme

¼ teaspoon dried sage

½ teaspoon sea salt

¼ teaspoon ground black pepper

One 16-ounce package whole wheat spaghetti

One 24-ounce jar of your favorite organic tomato sauce (no sugar added)

½ cup shredded raw Parmesan cheese

Chopped fresh Italian parsley (optional)

Preheat the oven to 350°F.

Mix together the turkey, egg, and seasonings in a bowl. Form the mixture into meatballs, using 2 level tablespoons for each; place on a greased baking sheet and bake until cooked through, about 20 minutes.

Cook the spaghetti according to the package directions.

Remove the turkey meatballs from the oven and place them in a pot with the tomato sauce. Heat until warm.

Serve the meatballs over the spaghetti and topped with Parmesan cheese.

LENTIL PASTA
with Kale Pesto

There could never be too much kale in my life. Thankfully, my daughter loves to eat it too. Like mother, like daughter. For a more substantial dish, this pasta would be great tossed with blanched green beans or broccoli florets.

Makes 4 servings
Prep Time: 10 minutes
Cook Time: 9 minutes

4 cups (packed) chopped, stemmed curly kale

¾ cup extra-virgin olive oil

½ cup toasted walnuts

⅓ cup grated raw Parmesan cheese

Juice of ½ lemon

3 garlic cloves, peeled

½ teaspoon sea salt

Grated zest of 1 lemon

8 ounces lentil pasta

Blend the kale, oil, nuts, cheese, lemon, garlic, salt, and zest in a food processor until the pesto is smooth.

Cook the pasta according to the package directions. Drain, reserving 1 cup cooking liquid.

Pour at least ½ cup pesto over the cooked pasta and toss to combine. Toss with enough reserved cooking liquid to moisten. Season with salt and pepper and serve, refrigerating any remaining pesto for up to one week.

COCONUT CURRY VEGETABLES
with Saffron Rice

If you're going meatless a few nights or more a week, you'll find this dish so warm and comforting. I'll sometimes mix up the vegetables with whatever I have on hand—the recipe is pretty versatile.

Serves 4 servings
Prep Time: 20 minutes
Cook Time: 20 minutes

1 tablespoon coconut oil
1 small yellow onion, diced
2-inch piece fresh ginger root, minced
2 tablespoons curry powder
1 garlic clove, minced
1 large zucchini, diced
1 large yellow squash, diced
2 carrots, sliced
1 head of broccoli, cut into 1-inch pieces (about 4 cups total)
1 Yukon gold potato, unpeeled, cut into ½-inch pieces
½ teaspoon sea salt
1¾ cups coconut milk or one 13.5-ounce can coconut milk
Black pepper to taste

Heat the oil in a large, deep skillet over medium heat. Add the onion, ginger, and curry powder and saute for 5 minutes, then add the garlic and saute for 2 minutes more.

Next add the zucchini, squash, carrots, broccoli, potato, and sea salt and cook for 4 to 5 minutes.

Add the coconut milk, stirring to combine. Cover and bring to a low simmer. Cook for 12 to 15 minutes, or until the potatoes are fork tender.

To make the Saffron Rice: Bring 2 cups of water to boil in a pot. Add the butter, saffron, turmeric, and salt, allowing the butter to melt. Add the rice; cover and simmer for roughly 15 minutes, or until liquid has evaporated.

Serve the vegetable curry over the saffron rice.

SAFFRON RICE

1 teaspoon butter
Pinch of saffron threads
½ teaspoon ground turmeric
½ teaspoon salt
1 cup basmati rice

MY MOM'S DAHL

This is the dahl my mom makes all the time. I'll have it just as a plain soup or I'll add chopped kale sometimes. I really love dipping her Kale Pranthas in it.

Makes 4 servings
Prep Time: 15 minutes
Cook Time: 35 minutes

½ cup red lentils
½ cup yellow lentils
2 tablespoons olive oil
1 zucchini, diced
1 teaspoon sea salt
1 teaspoon ground turmeric
1 tablespoon minced and peeled fresh ginger root
2 tablespoons ghee
1 teaspoon whole cumin seeds
1 tablespoon minced garlic
1 small yellow onion, diced
½ teaspoon paprika
1 tomato, diced
¼ teaspoon ground fennel

Wash all the lentils 3 times and let them soak.

Heat the oil in a pot over medium heat. Add the zucchini and cook for 2 to 3 minutes.

Add the lentils to the pot and cook for 2 to 3 minutes.

Add the salt, turmeric, and 2 cups filtered water; cover and bring to a boil.

Add the ginger; reduce the heat, cover, and let simmer for 10 minutes.

Heat the ghee in a separate pot over medium heat. Add the cumin, garlic, and onion. Sauté 4 to 5 minutes, or until the onions are translucent.

Add the paprika and tomato to the onion mixture and sauté for 5 minutes.

Pour the onion mixture into the pot with the lentil mixture along with ½ cup filtered water and the ground fennel. Bring to a boil, then reduce the heat and simmer uncovered for 5 minutes to allow the flavors to meld.

My mom makes this and the Curried Cauliflower (page 218), Kale Pranthas (page 228), and one of my favorite desserts, delicious Carrot Halwa (page 266) as one big meal. It's amazing.

PERFECT CHICKEN ENCHILADAS

Homemade enchilada sauce is a must if you're going to make enchiladas. You've got to make the whole enchilada, right? My version incorporates healthy olive oil and spices, unlike those canned versions filled with soybean oil, white sugar, and MSG-like additives. And, dare I say, it tastes a zillion times better too. This is one of my husband's favorite dishes.

Makes 4 to 6 servings
Prep Time: 20 minutes
Cook Time: 65 minutes

8 to 10 ounces skinless boneless chicken breasts, cooked and shredded

1 cup pinto beans, cooked and smashed (see slow cooker beans recipe on page 225)

1½ cup raw goat cheddar cheese, shredded, divided

½ cup diced yellow onion

6 large sprouted wheat tortillas

1 cup chopped fresh cilantro

ENCHILADA SAUCE

1 tablespoon olive oil

1 cup chopped yellow onion

2 garlic cloves, minced

1 tablespoon ground cumin

1 tablespoon chili powder

¼ teaspoon cayenne pepper

3 cups chopped ripe tomatoes, or a jar of pureed tomatoes

2 jalapeño peppers, seeded and diced

1 dried ancho chile, stemmed, seeded, and broken into pieces

Preheat the oven to 350°F.

To make the enchilada sauce, heat the oil in a heavy medium saucepan over medium heat.

Add the onion and cook for 4 to 5 minutes. Add the garlic and spices and cook for 1 minute.

Add the tomatoes, ¼ cup filtered water, jalapeño, and ancho chile and bring to a boil. Reduce the heat and simmer for 15 minutes, or until the vegetables are tender, stirring frequently. Puree the mixture using a counter blender or immersion blender. Season with salt to taste. Spread ½ cup of the sauce over the bottom of a baking dish until evenly coated. Set the remaining sauce aside.

To assemble the enchiladas, place the chicken, beans, 1 cup cheese, and onion in a bowl and mix to combine. Fill each tortilla with about ½ cup of the mixture. Roll up the tortillas over the filling and place in the baking pan on top of the enchilada sauce. Pour the remaining sauce over the enchiladas and top with cilantro and remaining ½ cup cheese. Cover and bake until heated through, about 30 minutes.

LEMON HERB SNAPPER

This buttery baked snapper is super simple and so delicious. I like to pair it with rice made with bone broth and steamed veggies for an easy weeknight dinner.

Makes 4 servings
Prep Time: 10 minutes
Cook Time: 15 minutes

¼ cup unsalted butter, softened
2 tablespoons fresh thyme leaves
¼ teaspoon sea salt
⅛ teaspoon ground black pepper
Four 4-ounce wild-caught snapper fillets
8 thin lemon slices

Preheat the oven to 400°F.

Mix together the butter, thyme, salt, and pepper in a small bowl and set aside.

Place the snapper on a parchment-lined rimmed baking sheet. Rub each fillet with some of the butter mix and top each with 2 lemon slices.

Bake for 12 to 15 minutes, or until desired doneness.

SWEET ASIAN SALMON
with Braised Red Cabbage

This Asian-inspired salmon is incredibly delicious paired with braised red cabbage. You can also serve it with roasted veggies, rice, or quinoa. The possibilities are virtually endless. The cabbage keeps for several days in the fridge, and is great reheated.

Makes 4 servings
Prep Time: 10 minutes
Cook Time: 20 minutes

¼ cup low-sodium tamari
2 tablespoons mirin
2 tablespoons coconut sugar
2 tablespoons minced fresh ginger root
2 tablespoons minced garlic
1 pound wild-caught salmon, skin on
2 scallions, chopped (for garnish)

BRAISED RED CABBAGE

1 tablespoon butter or olive oil
2 garlic cloves, minced
3 whole allspice berries, crushed, or ¼ teaspoon ground allspice
½ large head of red cabbage, thinly sliced
2 green apples, diced
½ cup apple juice
1 tablespoon apple cider vinegar

Preheat the oven to 425°F.

Place the tamari, mirin, sugar, ginger, and garlic in a small saucepan over medium-high heat. Bring to a boil and simmer until reduced to ⅓ cup, about 5 to 7 minutes, stirring occasionally. Let cool.

Place the salmon, skin side down, in an oven-safe glass dish. Pour the marinade over and let sit for at least 1 hour or refrigerate up to 6 hours.

To make the Braised Red Cabbage: Melt the butter in a large saucepan over medium heat. Add the garlic and allspice and cook for 1 to 2 minutes. Add the cabbage, apples, and apple juice and cook for 20 minutes, stirring occasionally. Stir in the vinegar and cook for an additional 3 minutes. Season with salt and pepper.

Place the salmon in the oven and bake until just cooked through, about 15 to 20 minutes depending on the thickness of fish. Let rest for 2 to 5 minutes. Spoon the marinade back over the salmon and top with scallions before serving with the cabbage.

HEARTY VEGETABLE FRIED CAULIFLOWER RICE

Anytime I'm craving a quick dish that is full of vegetables, this savory fried rice is the ticket. It's hearty on its own, or sometimes I'll pair it with some salmon or chicken.

Makes 4 servings
Prep Time: 20 minutes
Cook Time: 11 minutes

1 head cauliflower, very coarsely chopped

2 tablespoons coconut oil

3 carrots, diced

½ yellow onion, diced

2 garlic cloves, peeled and minced

1 zucchini, diced

1 large egg, beaten

¼ cup low-sodium tamari, or more as needed

Sea salt and pepper to taste

¼ cup chopped parsley

½ cup toasted cashews

Working in batches, place the chopped cauliflower in a food processor and pulse until a rice-like consistency has formed. Set aside.

Heat the oil in a large, deep skillet over medium heat. Add the carrots, onion, and garlic and cook for 2 to 3 minutes. Add the cauliflower and zucchini and cook for 4 to 5 minutes. Add the egg and cook 1 to 2 minutes, stirring to combine. Pour the tamari over the cauliflower mix and season with salt and pepper. Continue to cook for 2 to 3 minutes for the flavors to meld.

Serve with chopped parsley and cashews on top.

SLOPPY JOE POCKETS

Unlike most sloppy joes, these are packed with veggies and stuffed inside a pita instead of a heavy bun. This helps to keep all the goodness inside instead of on your lap! They're so fun to eat and the whole family will love them.

Makes 4 servings
Prep Time: 15 minutes
Cook Time: 15 minutes

2 tablespoons olive oil

1 large red pepper, diced

1 green pepper, diced

2 stalks celery, diced

1 yellow onion, diced

3 garlic cloves, minced

1 pound ground turkey

One 6-ounce can tomato paste

2 teaspoons Dijon mustard

1 tablespoon honey

1 tablespoon chili powder

2 teaspoons apple cider vinegar

½ teaspoon sea salt

Ground black pepper to taste

4 whole wheat pita breads, cut crosswise in half

Heat the oil in a heavy large deep skillet over medium heat. Add the bell peppers, celery, onion, and garlic, then add the turkey and sauté for 4 to 5 minutes to soften the vegetables.

Add the tomato paste, mustard, honey, chili powder, vinegar, and salt, then mix in 2 cups filtered water. Cook until the turkey is cooked through and the mixture thickens, about 10 minutes. Season with pepper.

Toast the pita halves for about 30 seconds over an open flame or in a skillet to heat through, turning often with tongs.

Spoon ½ cup filling into each pita pocket and serve.

FINLEY'S PULLED PORK BBQ

My husband, Finley, is an amazing cook, but he doesn't do anything simple. He tends to pick complex recipes that take him hours to make. Thankfully, I get to eat what he makes, and this pulled pork recipe he spends all day on is incredible. I grew up with barbecue here in the South and am so happy I can enjoy this homemade recipe. Don't be shy about making a big batch; this pork freezes great, and warms up nicely for sandwiches and slaw anytime.

Makes 20 servings
Prep Time: 30 minutes
Cook Time: 6 hours

Approximately 5 pounds boneless pork butt
3 chunks of hickory wood
¼ cup yellow mustard

Place all the spices for the pork rub in an airtight jar and shake to combine.

Combine all the ingredients for the basting juice in a bowl and place in the fridge.

Wash the pork butt and dry completely with paper towels. Coat the entire pork butt with a thin layer of yellow mustard, then massage the pork rub onto the pork butt. Place in a covered glass dish and store in the fridge overnight.

Heat a charcoal smoker to 275°F.

Place a few hickory chunks on the grill and wait until the smoke has changed from white to gray (approximately 30 minutes).

Insert a thermometer into the pork butt and place it in the smoker over a large drip pan.

Open the smoker and pour a few spoonfuls of basting juice over the meat once every hour. Cook until the thermometer reaches 195°F to 200°F (approximately 1 to 1¼ hour per pound).

Once done, remove the pork butt from the smoker, wrap in wax-free parchment paper, and then wrap in aluminum foil. Let rest for 1 hour.

Unwrap the pork, place it in a large square glass dish or on a cutting board and shred the meat to a pulled pork consistency.

To make the vinegar sauce, place all the ingredients in a pot and bring to a low simmer. Cook for 12 to 15 minutes to combine the flavors.

Add the sauce to the pulled pork and enjoy! It's great with pickles (see recipe page 235), on a bun with sauce and slaw, or eaten by itself.

PORK RUB

1 tablespoon sweet paprika
2 tablespoons coconut sugar
1 tablespoon coarse sea salt
2 teaspoons ground black pepper
2 teaspoons chili powder
2 teaspoons garlic powder
2 teaspoons onion powder
½ teaspoon celery seeds
¼ teaspoon cayenne pepper

VINEGAR SAUCE

1½ cups apple cider vinegar
1½ tablespoons brown sugar
2 tablespoons ketchup
2 teaspoons hot sauce
1½ tablespoons red pepper flakes
3 teaspoons sea salt
1 teaspoon ground black pepper
Pinch of cayenne pepper

BASTING JUICE

2 cups apple cider vinegar
½ cup apple juice
1 tablespoon sea salt
1 teaspoon ground black pepper
1 teaspoon red pepper flakes
1 yellow onion, chopped
1 jalapeño pepper, sliced

chapter 8

SIDES

Sometimes these "sides" end up taking over most of my plate. There's no reason to limit yourself when it comes to extra servings of vegetables, right?

GARLIC SAUTÉED BOK CHOY

Add a big heaping spoonful of this to your plate, as it packs some serious nutritional punch! Bok choy is a cruciferous vegetable, which helps protect the body from multiple types of cancer. It's also an incredible source of antioxidants that zap free radicals, which can lead to cancer, neurodegenerative disease, and other disorders. The best part? Preparing it with garlic and lemon juice is simple and flavorful, which makes it a great complement to almost any meal. Bonus tip: This is an easy green to grow in a garden. Harley loves to pick it and later eat this dish.

Makes 4 servings
Prep Time: 5 minutes
Cook Time: 7 minutes

1 tablespoon olive oil
2 garlic cloves, minced
3 heads bok choy, chopped
½ lemon, juiced
Sea salt and ground black pepper

Heat the oil in a sauté pan over medium heat. Add the garlic and cook for 1 to 2 minutes.

Add the bok choy and cook for 4 to 5 minutes, or until softened.

Take off the heat and drizzle with lemon juice. Season with salt and pepper.

CILANTRO RICE SALAD

This salad is zesty, really FRESH, and complements almost any meal! It also happens to be one of the simplest recipes in the world. It's just as easy to make as those boxes of Rice-A-Roni, but without the nasty additives—and it tastes a million times better too. Even if you are a beginner cook, this is a meal or side dish that will impress your friends and family with very little effort!

Makes 4 servings
Prep Time: 5 minutes
Cook Time: 30 minutes

1 tablespoon coconut oil or butter

½ yellow onion, diced

2 garlic cloves, minced

1 cup uncooked brown basmati rice or quinoa

2 cups chicken broth or vegetable stock

½ cup or more chopped cilantro

1 lime, zested and juiced

Sea salt and ground black pepper to taste

Heat the oil in a pot over medium heat. Add the onion and garlic and cook for 2 to 3 minutes. Add the dry rice and cook for an additional minute, stirring so the rice doesn't burn.

Add the broth, cover, and turn the heat to a low simmer. Cook until the liquid has evaporated and the rice is cooked through, about 25 to 30 minutes.

Take off the heat and stir in the cilantro, lime zest, and lime juice. Season with salt and pepper.

QUINOA TABBOULEH

When I buy a few bunches of parsley at the store, I almost always get a "What are you going to do with all that?" Parsley is just magical. I've become absolutely addicted to the way I feel after I eat this dish—my energy soars, my appetite is fulfilled, and I feel light, beautiful, and radiant. I never realized that food could have such an impact on my mind and body before I started basing my diet on the most nutrient-dense foods on the planet. This is what happens when you realize that food is medicine. And this salad is exactly that!

Makes 4 servings
Prep Time: 15 minutes
Cook Time: 30 minutes

1 cup dry quinoa, rinsed and drained
½ large bunch of parsley, chopped
1 cup cherry tomatoes, cut in half
¼ red onion, diced
⅓ cup mint leaves, chopped
2 tablespoons extra-virgin olive oil
Juice of 1 lemon
1 garlic clove, minced
½ teaspoon sea salt
¼ teaspoon ground black pepper

Optional Toppings

Goat's milk feta cheese
Sliced avocado

Cook the quinoa according to the package instructions. Drain and cool.

Place all the ingredients except the toppings in a bowl and mix well to combine. Add desired toppings before serving.

BAKED SWEET POTATOES

Sweet potatoes are so healthy, I eat them at least once a week, if not more. They are packed with anti-oxidants and are excellent for your gut health. I serve these with my Foolproof Roasted Chicken (see recipe page 185), along with a big salad to round out the perfect meal, even on the busiest nights.

Makes 4 servings
Prep Time: 5 minutes
Cook Time: 35 minutes

4 medium sweet potatoes
2 tablespoons olive oil
4 teaspoons butter
Sea salt and ground black pepper

Preheat the oven to 350°F.

Rub each sweet potato with olive oil and place on a parchment-lined baking sheet. Bake for 30 to 35 minutes or until fork tender.

Cool slightly. Make a slit in each sweet potato and add 1 teaspoon butter and a sprinkle of salt and pepper.

VEENA'S GOBI
(CURRIED CAULIFLOWER)

My mom has been making this cauliflower for as long as I can remember. The scent of all these incredible warming spices on the stove just feels like home.

Makes 4 to 6 servings
Prep Time: 10 minutes
Cook Time: 16 to 18 minutes

3 tablespoons olive oil
1 teaspoon whole cumin seeds
1 tablespoon minced fresh ginger root
One 2-pound head cauliflower, cut into florets
1 teaspoon ground turmeric
½ teaspoon paprika
½ teaspoon sea salt

Heat the oil in a large deep skillet over medium heat.

Add the cumin seeds and cook for 30 seconds.

Add the ginger and cook for an additional 30 seconds.

Add the remaining ingredients and cook for 4 to 5 minutes.

Reduce the heat to low, cover, and simmer until the cauliflower is crisp-tender, stirring occasionally, about 10 minutes.

BRUSSELS SPROUTS WITH BEETS AND CARROTS

I make this for my family during the holidays and it's always a hit. But it's a great all-around side dish for any time of year, one that tastes like you spent much more time in the kitchen than you actually did. Shhhh. Don't worry, I won't tell anyone.

Makes 4 to 6 servings
Prep Time: 10 minutes
Cook Time: 30 minutes

1 large beet, peeled and chopped into cubes

4 cups chopped cruciferous vegetables (cauliflower, brussels sprouts, and/or broccoli)

2 large carrots, chopped

1 large garlic bulb, broken up into cloves and peeled

¼ teaspoon sea salt

Ground black pepper to taste

2 teaspoons coconut oil

Preheat the oven to 375°F.

Place all the ingredients on a sheet pan and toss to combine. Bake for 30 minutes or until the vegetables are fork tender.

CAULIFLOWER MAC 'N' CHEESE

I originally developed this recipe for a family that was addicted to heavily processed boxed mac 'n' cheese. They had two kids, one on the way, and I wanted to arm them with the most delicious, satisfying homemade recipe that was also good for them. The kids could not stop eating this—and didn't notice the star ingredient, cauliflower, at all.

Makes 8 servings
Prep Time: 10 minutes
Cook Time: 20 minutes

One 16-ounce package sprouted whole wheat or spelt pasta noodles

1 head cauliflower, chopped

2 tablespoons butter

12 ounces goat's milk mild cheddar cheese, shredded

Sea salt and ground black pepper to taste

⅛ teaspoon nutmeg

Cook the pasta according to the package directions.

While the pasta is cooking, steam the cauliflower in a large pot filled with 1 to 2 cups of water.

Grate the cauliflower using a hand grater or pulse in a food processor.

Combine the cauliflower and the pasta. Mix in the butter, cheese, and seasonings. Serve.

SLOW COOKER BEANS

Top these slow-cooked beans with avocado, sour cream, hot sauce, and cheese. Prepare them in the morning, and they'll be ready and waiting at the end of the day. These beans can be frozen and reheated for later use in different dishes such as the Perfect Chicken Enchiladas (see recipe on page 196).

Makes 4 servings
Prep Time: 10 minutes
Cook Time: 8 hours

One 16-ounce package black beans or pinto beans
1 large yellow onion, cut in half
2 garlic cloves, minced
1 jalapeño pepper, seeded and diced
2 teaspoons ground cumin

Optional Toppings

Avocado
Sour cream
Cilantro
Lime juice
Hot sauce
Grated cheese

Soak the beans for at least 8 hours or overnight. Drain and rinse.

Place all the ingredients in a slow cooker and pour in approximately 6 cups water, enough to cover the beans by 1 inch. Cook on high for 8 hours.

Drain the excess liquid or reserve, based on your preference. Season with salt to taste and add toppings as desired.

RAINBOW POTATO FRIES

I love fries. They are one of my favorite foods besides cake. But I hate getting them from most restaurants because I know they are being fried in unhealthy oils. This olive oil baked version is much healthier. You can use any kind of potato or mix different types together like I do for a "rainbow" version.

Makes 4 servings
Prep Time: 5 minutes
Cook Time: 20 minutes

1 large Yukon gold potato, cut into
2- to 3-inch-long strips

1 large sweet potato, cut into
2- to 3-inch-long strips

1 large purple potato, cut into
2- to 3-inch-long strips

3 to 4 tablespoons olive oil

Sea salt and ground black pepper
to taste

Preheat the oven to 375°F.

Toss the potatoes with olive oil, salt, and pepper. Place on a mesh baking rack and bake for 25 minutes, tossing at the half way point. Serve with ketchup or your favorite dip.

KALE PRANTHAS

My mom created these using kale that she grows in her garden. These are absolutely amazing and *you need to try them*. I will eat four of these in one sitting; I literally can't stop. There's not much else I can say. Harley enjoys eating bite-size pieces with grass-fed butter on top.

Makes 8 servings
Prep Time: 45 minutes
plus resting time
Cook Time: 20 minutes

2.5 ounces baby kale or stemmed regular kale

3 cups whole wheat pastry flour, divided

½ teaspoon sea salt

3 teaspoons olive oil, divided, plus more oil for rolling

8 teaspoons grass-fed butter or ghee

Place 1 cup water in a pot and bring to a boil. Add the kale and steam for 5 to 7 minutes, or until almost tender.

Using tongs, transfer the kale to a blender or mini food processor and puree, stopping occasionally to scrape down the sides. Let cool.

Place 2 cups flour and ½ teaspoon salt in a large bowl and mix to combine.

Add the cooled kale puree and mix. Add about 1 cup of filtered water, a little at a time, mixing with your hands as you go and adding just enough until a soft dough has formed.

Knead the dough for 2 to 3 minutes. My mom does this by making a fist and pressing down on the dough, turning and flipping it several times while pressing down.

Add 1 teaspoon oil and rub around the dough. Cover with a towel for 10 minutes or up to 2 hours if you have time (2 hours is best).

After letting the dough rest, knead it once more for 1 minute. Divide the dough into 8 balls, roughly the size of a large ice-cream scoop.

Heat the remaining 2 teaspoons oil in a cast-iron pan over medium-low heat.

Place the remaining 1 cup of flour on a plate.

Take one of the dough balls and pat it down on the plate of flour until it's evenly covered. Shake off excess.

Roll each ball into a thin tortilla shape (about 6 inches round).

Drizzle ¼ teaspoon olive oil over the tortilla along with a small sprinkle of flour. Fold both ends on top of one another like an envelope. Add a bit more olive oil and fold again to make a square shape.

Coat in flour again and shake off the excess. Roll into the same thin tortilla shape as before.

Place in the cast-iron pan and cook for 1 to 2 minutes per side, or until golden brown.

Add roughly 1 teaspoon grass-fed butter or ghee to the top of each and serve. Repeat with the remaining dough.

HOMEMADE FLOUR TORTILLAS

Most store-bought tortillas have awful ingredients, so I had to make my own. But I wanted them to taste just like a restaurant's so I went with white flour. The same recipe could be made with whole wheat flour or spelt. Warning: Once you start making your own, you'll never go back—they are addictive.

Makes 12 tortillas
Prep Time: 20 minutes
Cook Time: 30 minutes

3 cups all-purpose flour
1 teaspoon fine sea salt
4½ tablespoons olive oil
1⅛ cups filtered water

Mix the flour and salt in a bowl. Add the oil and filtered water and stir gently until most of the flour is mixed in (don't overmix).

Knead the dough in a bowl, folding roughly 10 times. Let rest for 15 minutes.

Divide the dough into 12 equal balls and place on an oiled plate.

Heat a cast-iron griddle or skillet to medium and make sure that the surface is clean.

Press a dough ball in your tortilla press and then carefully place the raw pressed tortilla onto the griddle. If you don't have a tortilla press, roll out the dough into 7-inch rounds between sheets of parchment paper.

Cook for approximately 40 seconds on the first side, then flip over and cook for 40 seconds on the second side. Flip over once more and cook for another minute. The tortilla should bubble and puff up in spots. Repeat the process with the remaining dough. Wrap the cooked tortillas in a clean kitchen towel and cover to keep warm.

GARLIC HERB ASPARAGUS ROLL-UPS

These taste even more incredible than they look. That herb butter smothered on pastry-covered asparagus . . . mmm mmm . . . heaven on a plate.

Makes 4 servings
Prep Time: 10 minutes
Cook Time: 16 minutes

One 14-ounce package pastry dough, thawed
1 bunch of asparagus

GARLIC HERB BUTTER

¼ cup melted butter
1 garlic clove, minced
½ teaspoon Italian seasoning

Preheat the oven to 350°F.

Lay out the pastry dough and cut it into 1-inch strips lengthwise.

Roll each strip around an asparagus spear. Continue until all the spears have been wrapped. Set on a parchment-lined baking sheet.

For the Garlic Herb Butter, mix all the ingredients in a small bowl. Brush the butter onto the tops of the pastry dough. Be generous!

Bake for 14 to 16 minutes or until golden brown. Serve immediately.

FERMENTED PICKLES

Almost every jar of pickles at the store is packed in artificially colored vinegar and risky preservatives. I avoid all that nonsense, and pack in a one-two punch by making fermented pickles at home. I do my best to eat fermented foods every day, as it is a great way to get healthy bacteria into your gut, which promotes good health in so many ways. I love to add these pickles to homemade turkey burgers, alongside Finley's Pulled Pork BBQ (see recipe on page 206), and of course, on my famous "Chick-fil-A" Sandwich (see recipe on page 180).

Makes 1 quart
Prep Time: 15 minutes, plus 72 to 96 hours for fermentation

1 pound pickling cucumbers
(4- to 6-inch cucumbers)
4 garlic cloves, peeled and sliced
1 to 2 tablespoons chopped
fresh dill
2 bay leaves
½ teaspoon black peppercorns
½ teaspoon mustard seeds
3 tablespoons apple cider vinegar
1½ tablespoons sea salt

Wash the cucumbers under cold water to remove any dirt. Slice them lengthwise into 4 to 6 spears per cucumber.

In a 32-ounce sterilized glass jar, add the sliced garlic, fresh dill, bay leaves, peppercorns, mustard seeds, and vinegar. Place the cucumber spears in the jar.

Heat 3 cups of water in a pot over medium heat. Add the salt and cook until dissolved.

Pour the salted water into the jar with the cucumbers, leaving roughly 1 to 2 inches of room on top. Seal the jar.

Place the jar in a cool, dark place for 3 to 4 days, checking after the third day. Once you start to see small bubbles and the water begins to get cloudy, you can place the pickles in the refrigerator to continue to ferment. Store in the refrigerator for up to 2 to 3 months.

chapter 9

DESSERTS

If you know me, you know I love dessert. Seriously, it's my favorite part of any meal, and I have something sweet EVERY. SINGLE. DAY. My sweet tooth, however, is usually satisfied by something naturally sweet and relatively low in sugar, or at the very least it will be made with nontoxic ingredients.

FOREVER COOKIES

These little babies are a creation that I made up several years ago when I was trying to figure out the recipe for a vegan Earth Fare cookie that always calls my name at the end of my shopping trip. I think I have shopped there maybe twice without getting one. One of those times, the store was out of them and the other was because I knew I had just baked a batch of these myself. I named these cookies "Forever" because they are so darn good that you will wish you were eating them . . . like . . . forever.

Makes 18 to 20 cookies
Prep Time: 10 minutes
Cook Time: 15 minutes

1 ripe banana, cut into small pieces
4 dates, chopped
4 prunes, chopped
¼ cup coconut oil, melted
1 teaspoon vanilla extract
2 cups rolled oats
⅔ cup nut meal
½ cup unsweetened coconut flakes
½ teaspoon ground cinnamon
½ teaspoon sea salt
1 teaspoon baking powder
7 ounces dark chocolate, chopped into pieces

Preheat the oven to 350°F.

Combine the banana, dates, prunes, coconut oil, and vanilla in a blender and blend until smooth.

Combine the remaining ingredients in a large bowl and mix well.

Pour the blender mixture into the dry mixture and stir until the batter is moist.

Place the dough in the fridge or freezer for at least 15 minutes to harden.

Scoop the dough using an ice-cream scoop onto a parchment-lined baking sheet.

Bake the cookies for 12 to 15 minutes. Let cool.

ALMOND BUTTER BROWNIES

My classic almond butter brownies are always a hit. The trick is not eating them all in one sitting! Whether you eat them gooey hot out of the oven or freeze them into little bites, these suckers are deadly addictive. Don't say I didn't warn you.

Makes 8 servings
Prep Time: 5 minutes
Cook Time: 25 minutes

1 cup almond butter
1 egg
½ teaspoon sea salt
½ teaspoon baking soda
½ cup coconut sugar
½ teaspoon vanilla extract
½ cup chopped dark chocolate

Preheat the oven to 350°F.

Grease an 8 x 8-inch baking dish or line the bottom with parchment paper.

Mix all the ingredients except the dark chocolate chunks until smooth.

Fold in the chocolate chunks and pour the batter into the prepared baking dish.

Bake the brownies until they are golden brown, about 25 minutes.

Cool the brownies for at least 10 minutes before cutting.

RASPBERRY THUMBPRINT COOKIES

These festive cookies are super fun to make for the holidays, but I'll make them any time of the year. They look a little fancy, but only take about 15 minutes of your time to put together. Get your kids involved—they'll love to press in their thumb and spoon in the raspberry filling!

Makes 12 to 15 cookies
Prep Time: 15 minutes
Cook Time: 12 minutes

¼ cup coconut oil, melted
½ cup coconut sugar
1 egg
1 tablespoon vanilla extract
2 cups almond flour
½ teaspoon baking powder
¼ teaspoon sea salt

RASPBERRY CHIA JAM

1 cup fresh raspberries
1 tablespoon chia seeds
1 to 2 teaspoons honey or maple syrup, if desired

Preheat the oven to 350°F.

To make the chia jam, place all the ingredients in a blender and blend until smooth. If you need more liquid for the ingredients to fully combine, add 1 to 2 tablespoons of filtered water. Place in a glass jar in the refrigerator to allow the chia seeds to expand, at least 1 hour or overnight.

To make the cookies, whisk together the oil, sugar, egg, and vanilla. Mix together the flour and salt in a separate bowl. Slowly pour the dry ingredients into the wet ingredients and mix well.

Scoop the cookie dough into 1-inch balls and place on a parchment-lined cookie sheet. Make a thumbprint in the center of each ball roughly ½ inch thick. Fill the indent with 1 teaspoon chia jam.

Bake the cookies for 12 to 15 minutes, or until slightly browned on the edges. Let cool.

GOJI BERRY DROPS

This is a recipe that my best friend, Nicole, shared with me several years ago. The combination of flavors in these treats is deadly! The smooth texture of the chocolate against the chewiness of the goji berries married with the crunch of the almonds and spike of sea salt is an EXPLOSION in your mouth. If you're not big on baking, no worries—you can throw this treat together in a matter of minutes without turning on an oven, and you need only four ingredients!

Makes 40 drops
Prep Time: 25 minutes, plus 1 hour to harden

20 ounces chocolate chips
4 ounces goji berries
8 ounces almonds, chopped
¼ teaspoon sea salt, plus additional for sprinkling

Fill a small pot with ½ cup water and heat to a simmer.

Place a large bowl on top of the pot, creating a double boiler.

Fill the bowl with the chocolate and slowly melt.

Once all the chocolate is melted, stir in the berries, almonds, and salt.

Use a tablespoon-size ice-cream scoop or spoon to drop the mixture onto a parchment-lined baking sheet.

Top each drop with a small sprinkle of sea salt (and a few almonds and goji berries if you like).

Refrigerate to allow the drops to cool.

HEALTHIER BIRTHDAY CAKE

I made my daughter this special one-of-a-kind cake with organic ingredients for her first birthday. It turned out so delicious, I plan to make it time and time again for birthdays and other celebrations! The base is made with organic oat flour, for which you can simply grind any kind of oats in a spice grinder or buy it prepackaged. This is adapted from Kristine's Kitchen.

Makes 6 servings
Prep Time: 10 minutes
Cook Time: 20 minutes

1 cup oat flour
½ teaspoon baking powder
½ teaspoon baking soda
½ teaspoon ground cinnamon
⅛ teaspoon sea salt
1 ripe banana, peeled
⅓ cup unsweetened applesauce
¼ cup coconut milk
1 egg
1 teaspoon vanilla extract
¼ cup pure maple syrup
Butter and oat flour for the pan

FROSTING

1 teaspoon vanilla extract
8 tablespoons butter
1 cup powdered sugar

Preheat the oven to 350°F.

Butter a mini tiered cake pan and dust it with oat flour.

Whisk together the dry ingredients in a large bowl and set aside.

Blend the banana, applesauce, coconut milk, egg, vanilla, and maple syrup together in a separate bowl.

Pour the wet ingredients into the dry ingredients and mix until just combined.

Pour the batter into your cake pan. Bake for 20 minutes, or until a toothpick inserted in the center comes out clean.

Let the cake cool in the pan for 30 minutes before removing and cool completely before frosting.

To make the frosting, cream together all the ingredients until smooth.

ALMOND BUTTER FREEZER FUDGE

The best thing about this fudge (other than the fact that it tastes just heavenly!) is that the nutritional profile does not resemble dessert at all. It's made with real food ingredients and none of that sweetened condensed milk, marshmallow creme, heaps of white sugar, and other nasty ingredients found in most fudge. A one-inch square of this fudge has just the right amount of sweetness, fat, and protein to seriously satisfy your sweet tooth, unlike traditional desserts that cause you to overindulge. And I just love the fact that it is stored and eaten right out of the freezer.

Makes 20 pieces
Prep Time: 1 hour 15 minutes

1 cup almond butter
4 tablespoons coconut oil
1½ tablespoons maple syrup
1 teaspoon vanilla extract
½ teaspoon sea salt
4 ounces dark chocolate, chopped

Cream all the ingredients together in a bowl, except for the chopped chocolate.

Pour the mixture into an 8 x 6-inch baking dish lined with parchment paper.

Top with the chopped chocolate and freeze for at least 2 hours.

Remove the baking dish from the freezer, and carefully remove the fudge from the dish by lifting the ends of the parchment paper.

Cut the fudge into 1-inch squares and store in the freezer separated by parchment paper.

COOKIES 'N' CREAM COCONUT ICE CREAM

If there's one thing that gets me off my routine, it's ice cream. I love it! That's why I created this recipe, so I can enjoy ice cream all the time without sacrificing how I feel, my health, or the way I look. This coconut milk ice cream is actually quite healthful, but shhhh . . . no one will know!

Makes 10 servings
Prep Time: 25 minutes

One 13.5-ounce can full-fat coconut milk

3 frozen bananas or ½ cup coconut sugar

Pinch of sea salt

1 tablespoon vanilla extract

10 store-bought organic chocolate cookies, broken into pieces

Combine all the ingredients except the cookies in a blender and blend until smooth.

Pour the mixture into an ice cream machine and turn it on.

Mix for at least 20 minutes or until ice cream is formed.

Stir in the chopped cookies. This dessert is best served immediately.

8-MINUTE CANDY BAR

When you crave chocolate but don't want to eat the stuff filled with artificial ingredients sold at convenience stores, try this recipe. It's fast, fun, easy to make, and portable.

Makes 12 bars or 24 squares
Prep Time: 5 minutes plus refrigeration
Cook Time: 5 minutes

12 ounces dark chocolate chips

1 cup brown rice cereal or puffed quinoa

¾ cup almonds or peanuts chopped, divided

1 teaspoon vanilla extract

½ teaspoon sea salt

Place 1 cup of water in a small pot over medium heat. Set a heatproof bowl on top of the pot, creating a double boiler.

Add the chocolate to the bowl and stir until melted and warm to touch.

Take off the heat and mix in the cereal, ½ cup nuts, vanilla extract, and sea salt. Stir well to combine.

Pour the mixture into an 8 x 8-inch baking pan lined with parchment; smooth the top. Sprinkle the remaining ¼ cup nuts over. Refrigerate just until firm enough to cut but not completely set, about 1 hour. Lift the chocolate from the pan using the parchment as an aid. Cut into 12 bars or 24 squares.

LUSCIOUS LEMON BARS

These cool and tangy treats have just the right amount of sweetness. I love to pair them with a cup of hot herbal tea and find my happy place.

Makes 16 bars
Prep Time: 15 minutes
Cook Time: 25 minutes

Preheat the oven to 350°F.

For the crust, cream together the butter and sugar in a medium bowl. Add the flour and salt and mix until crumbly dough forms. Place the dough in a parchment-lined 8 x 8-inch baking pan and press out evenly.

For the filling, whisk together the eggs, honey, lemon juice, lemon zest, and coconut flour. Set aside.

Bake the crust for 12 minutes, or until lightly browned.

Pour the filling over the warm crust and bake for an additional 18 to 20 minutes, or until set.

Let cool, then store in the refrigerator. To serve, cut into bars and top with fresh raspberries, if desired.

CRUST

6 tablespoons butter or coconut oil
⅓ cup coconut sugar
1½ cups oat flour
¼ teaspoon sea salt

FILLING

4 large eggs
6 tablespoons raw honey
½ cup fresh lemon juice
1 tablespoon grated lemon zest
1 tablespoon coconut flour
½ cup raspberries (optional)

STRAWBERRY GINGER CRUMBLE

I love recipes like this healthy crumble. It's sweet and tart with just a small amount of coconut sugar added. You really don't need to add very much sugar to your desserts. This crumble is the absolute best with fresh organic strawberries from the farmers market!

Makes 4 servings
Prep Time: 10 minutes
Cook Time: 25 minutes

FILLING

2 cups sliced strawberries
1 to 2 tablespoons coconut sugar
1 tablespoon oat flour
1 teaspoon vanilla extract

CRUST

¾ cup oat flour
½ cup rolled oats
2 tablespoons coconut sugar
¼ teaspoon sea salt
½ teaspoon ground cinnamon
¼ teaspoon ground nutmeg
¼ teaspoon ground ginger
4 tablespoons butter or coconut oil

Preheat the oven to 375°F.

Mix all the ingredients for the filling in a bowl and transfer to an 8 x 8-inch baking dish.

For the crust, mix the flour, oats, sugar, salt, and spices in a bowl. Cut in the butter with a fork until the butter pieces are the size of peas.

Spoon the crust over the strawberry filling and bake for 25 to 30 minutes.

Serve the crumble hot with a scoop of ice cream, if desired.

ALMOND BISCOTTI

I love baking traditional sweets with better-for-you flours and ingredients. I send these to my friends for their birthdays or during the holidays as gifts and the response has been phenomenal. My friend Max from livingmaxwell.com said they were the best biscotti he had ever had!

Makes 12 cookies
Prep Time: 15 minutes
Cook Time: 45 minutes

1 cup of almonds
2 cups spelt flour
½ cup blanched almond flour
1 teaspoon baking powder
½ teaspoon sea salt
1 cup coconut sugar
4 tablespoons of grass-fed butter
3 eggs
2 teaspoons vanilla extract
Zest of 1 lemon
½ cup dried cranberries (optional)

Preheat the oven to 350°F.

Toast the almonds on a large baking pan for roughly 10 minutes as the oven is warming.

Place all the dry ingredients in a bowl and set aside.

Cream together the sugar and butter in a separate bowl using an electric mixer.

Add the eggs, vanilla, and lemon zest and mix well.

Add the flour mixture and mix until well combined.

Fold in the toasted almonds.

Split the dough into 2 uniform logs and place them on a large baking sheet lined with parchment paper. Bake for 35 minutes.

Cool for roughly 5 minutes, then cut each log into 6 slices.

Lay each slice flat back on the baking sheet, and bake for an additional 10 to 15 minutes per side, or until both sides are golden brown. Cool completely before serving.

FLOURLESS CHOCOLATE CHIP PEANUT BUTTER COOKIES

These cookies are a perfect treat because they don't contain any refined flour. They also freeze beautifully.

Makes 10 to 12 cookies
Prep Time: 10 minutes
Cook Time: 15 minutes

½ cup coconut sugar
2 teaspoons unsulphured molasses
1 egg, beaten
1 teaspoon vanilla extract
½ teaspoon baking soda
¼ teaspoon sea salt
1 cup peanut butter
4 ounces chocolate chips

Preheat the oven to 350°F. Line a large baking sheet with parchment paper.

Mix the sugar, molasses, egg, vanilla, baking soda, and salt in a large bowl.

Add the peanut butter and stir well to combine.

Fold in the chocolate chips.

Scoop 10 to 12 tablespoon-size balls onto the parchment-lined baking sheet.

Bake for 12 to 15 minutes, or longer if you like crispy cookies.

Place the cookies on a cooling rack and cool for 5 minutes.

3-MINUTE FRUIT SORBET

While we were traveling through Italy, my daughter fell in love with *sorbetto*. This fast version is great for weeknights, and best of all, doesn't require an ice-cream maker. Try making this recipe with strawberries, raspberries, or pineapple to change it up.

Makes 2 servings
Prep Time: 3 minutes

2 cups frozen mango
½ cup filtered water

Place the ingredients in a high-powered blender and blend until smooth.

ALL-FRUIT POPSICLES

These colorful treats are filled with only fresh fruit and a splash of coconut water. You'll never be tempted into buying those boxed popsicles full of crappy ingredients—like corn syrup—ever again!

Makes 8 servings
Prep Time: 10 minutes plus freezing

1 cup strawberries (ends trimmed), blueberries, raspberries, or other fruit of choice

½ cup coconut water

Place the ingredients in a blender and blend to combine.

Pour the mixture into popsicle molds and freeze for at least 4 hours.

MADELEINES

I love French bakeries, and this is one of the first treats I bought for Harley when we first went together. I had never seen her gobble up anything faster, so I knew I needed to buy a madeleine pan ASAP and get to work. I created this more healthful recipe using better-for-you flours and the result is equally delicious. Harley begs for these treats.

Makes 18 cookies
Prep Time: 10 minutes
Cook Time: 10 to 12 minutes

2 large eggs
⅔ cup coconut sugar
1 teaspoon vanilla extract
½ teaspoon grated lemon zest
Pinch of sea salt
½ cup unsalted butter, melted
½ cup spelt flour
½ cup almond flour

Preheat the oven to 375°F.

Beat together the eggs and sugar in a bowl just to blend. Add the vanilla, lemon zest, and salt and mix to combine.

With the mixer running, slowly add the melted butter until just combined.

Mix together the spelt flour and almond flour in a small bowl. Add the flour mixture to the bowl with the wet ingredients and stir until combined.

Spoon the batter by tablespoonfuls into a greased madeleine pan. Bake for 10 to 12 minutes, or until golden brown. Repeat with the remaining batter, buttering the pan between batches. Cool slightly, then remove the cookies from the pans. Cool the madeleines completely, then store in an airtight container.

HOMEMADE FIG NEWTONS

Have you seen the ingredients in traditional Fig Newtons? They are horrendous! But I am happy to say you can make this childhood treat at home with all the good ingredients. These are chewy and satisfying.

Makes 18 to 20 cookies
Prep Time: 15 minutes
Cook Time: 18 minutes

1 cup roughly chopped dried figs, stems removed

1 tablespoon raw honey

1 teaspoon grated orange zest

6 tablespoons unsalted butter, softened

½ cup coconut sugar

1 large egg

1 teaspoon vanilla extract

1½ cups whole wheat pastry flour

Preheat the oven to 350°F.

Soak the figs in enough hot water to cover for 10 to 12 minutes.

Drain and transfer the figs to a food processor. Add the honey and orange zest and pulse until pureed. Set aside.

Cream the butter and sugar together using a stand mixer. Add the egg and vanilla and mix until combined. Slowly add the flour and mix until a soft dough forms. Wrap the dough in plastic and chill 20 minutes.

Divide the dough in half; press each half into a narrow rectangle. Roll out each half on a sheet of parchment to a 12 x 4-inch rectangle, dusting with flour if necessary to keep from sticking.

Spread half the fig mixture in a long strip down one long side of each rectangle, leaving a ½-inch clean border. Fold the dough on top of itself and seal the edges.

Cut each log of dough crosswise into 8 to 10 cookies and place on a parchment-lined baking sheet. Bake for 15 to 18 minutes, or until golden brown. Cool, then store in an airtight container.

MY MOM'S CARROT HALWA

The more traditional recipe for carrot halwa takes about four hours to cook. My mom's version is super quick and can be done in an hour or less! This dessert is a mix between a pudding and a gooey cake—it's so satisfying.

Makes 6 to 8 servings
Prep Time: 20 minutes
Cook Time: 40 minutes

2 pounds carrots
1 cup half and half
½ cup butter or ghee
1 cup organic sugar
1 cup dry organic milk powder
½ teaspoon cardamom powder
½ cup unsweetened shredded coconut
½ cup sliced almonds or pistachios

Peel the carrots, then wash and dry them completely with a clean towel. Shred the carrots. If there is extra water on the carrots, the halwa will be watery.

Heat the half and half in a medium shallow pan over medium heat.

Add the carrots and cook for 20 minutes or until most of the half and half evaporates. Add the butter and sugar and continue to stir the mixture over medium heat for about 5 minutes, or until most of the liquid evaporates.

Add the dry milk and cardamom and stir well to combine. Add the coconut and nuts. Your carrot *halwa* will now be glistening with a beautiful orange color.

Serve hot garnished with more sliced nuts. Store in a glass dish in the fridge, and reheat leftovers for up to one week.

HARLEY'S STRAWBERRY CAKE

For Harley's third birthday, she requested a strawberry cake, and memories of the Duncan Hines boxed version filled my brain. I was not going to use a mix full of artificial ingredients, so I had to find a way to make it organic, beautiful, and delicious. This cake was a hit at her party, and guests commented that they liked it better than the bakery cupcakes I also served that day. Homemade is always more tasty, isn't it?

Makes 8 to 10 servings
Prep Time: 30 minutes
Cook Time: 25 minutes

16 ounces strawberries
2½ cups whole wheat pastry flour
2 teaspoons baking powder
½ teaspoon baking soda
1 teaspoon sea salt
¾ cup unsalted butter, softened
1½ cups coconut palm sugar
2 teaspoons vanilla extract
5 large egg whites, room temperature
1 cup coconut milk

STRAWBERRY FROSTING

One 1.2-ounce bag freeze-dried strawberries
8 ounces full-fat cream cheese, softened
½ cup unsalted butter, softened
3 cups organic powdered sugar
1 to 2 tablespoons coconut milk
1 teaspoon vanilla extract
Pinch of sea salt

Preheat the oven to 350°F.

Puree the strawberries in a blender. Transfer to a pot set over medium-low heat and cook until reduced to ⅔ cup, about 20 minutes, stirring occasionally. Set aside to cool.

Place the flour, baking powder, baking soda, and salt in a bowl and mix to combine.

Cream together the butter and sugar. Beat in the strawberry puree and vanilla. Beat in the egg whites, one at a time.

Add the dry ingredients and mix until just combined. Slowly beat in the milk just to blend.

Pour the batter into 2 greased parchment-lined 9-inch round baking pans. Bake for 20 minutes, or until a toothpick inserted into the center comes out clean. Cool the cakes in the pans set on racks.

To make the frosting, place the freeze-dried strawberries in a food processor and pulse to a powder.

Cream together the cream cheese and butter. Beat in the powdered sugar, coconut milk, vanilla, and salt. Add the strawberry powder and mix until fully incorporated.

To assemble, run a knife around the edges of the cake pans. Turn 1 cake out onto a plate or cake stand; peel off the parchment paper. Spread roughly 1 cup of frosting over the top of the cake, leaving a 1-inch border around the outside. Top with the second cake; peel off the parchment. Spread the remaining frosting over the top and sides of the cake. Top with fresh strawberries.

LEMON MUFFINS

These muffins have become a family favorite around here, but don't let the name "muffin" fool you. You could easily just call these cupcakes and make them for dessert. I discovered this recipe when visiting one of my favorite cafés, Flower Child. I love the bright, tart flavor and fluffy texture of this treat. Harley always asks for "just one more." It's also one of the few recipes I like to get my stand-mixer out for.

Makes 24 muffins
Prep Time: 15 minutes
Cook Time: 20 minutes

3 eggs
2 teaspoons vanilla extract
1½ cups evaporated cane sugar, divided
1 cup extra-virgin olive oil
4 tablespoons lemon juice (freshly juiced and strained)
4 teaspoons lemon zest
6 ounces coconut milk
1½ cups whole wheat pastry flour or gluten-free flour of choice
¾ teaspoon sea salt
¾ teaspoon baking soda
1 teaspoon baking powder

Preheat the oven to 315°F.

Combine eggs, vanilla, and 1 cup of sugar in a bowl or stand mixer. Whip for approximately 10 minutes or until fluffy.

In a separate bowl, combine oil, lemon juice, lemon zest, coconut milk, and ½ cup water. Slowly pour this into the bowl with the egg mixture and mix until just combined.

In a new bowl, combine flour, remaining ½ cup sugar, salt, baking soda, and baking powder.

Add the dry mixture into the wet mixture, about a third at a time, mixing after each time.

Place paper baking cups into a muffin tin and pour batter until ¾ of the way full. Bake for approximately 20 minutes or until a toothpick comes out clean. Cool completely before eating.

METRIC CONVERSION CHART

Standard Cup	Fine Powder (e.g., flour)	Grain (e.g., rice)	Granular (e.g., sugar)	Liquid Solids (e.g., butter)	Liquid (e.g., milk)
1	140 g	150 g	190 g	200 g	240 ml
¾	105 g	113 g	143 g	150 g	180 ml
⅔	93 g	100 g	125 g	133 g	160 ml
½	70 g	75 g	95 g	100 g	120 ml
⅓	47 g	50 g	63 g	67 g	80 ml
¼	35 g	38 g	48 g	50 g	60 ml
⅛	18 g	19 g	24 g	25 g	30 ml

Useful Equivalents for Cooking/Oven Temperatures

Process	Fahrenheit	Celsius	Gas Mark
Freeze Water	32° F	0° C	
Room Temperature	68° F	20° C	
Boil Water	212° F	100° C	
Bake	325° F	160° C	3
	350° F	180° C	4
	375° F	190° C	5
	400° F	200° C	6
	425° F	220° C	7
	450° F	230° C	8
Broil			Grill

Useful Equivalents for Liquid Ingredients by Volume

¼ tsp			1 ml
½ tsp			2 ml
1 tsp			5 ml
3 tsp	1 tbsp	½ fl oz	15 ml
	2 tbsp	⅛ cup	1 fl oz	30 ml
	4 tbsp	¼ cup	2 fl oz	60 ml
	5⅓ tbsp	⅓ cup	3 fl oz	80 ml
	8 tbsp	½ cup	4 fl oz	120 ml
	10⅔ tbsp	⅔ cup	5 fl oz	160 ml
	12 tbsp	¾ cup	6 fl oz	180 ml
	16 tbsp	1 cup	8 fl oz	240 ml
1 pt	2 cups	16 fl oz	480 ml
1 qt	4 cups	32 fl oz	960 ml

Useful Equivalents for Dry Ingredients by Weight

(To convert ounces to grams, multiply the number of ounces by 30.)

1 oz	1/16 lb	30 g
4 oz	¼ lb	120 g
8 oz	½ lb	240 g
12 oz	¾ lb	360 g
16 oz	1 lb	480 g

Useful Equivalents for Length

(To convert inches to centimeters, multiply the number of inches by 2.5.)

1 in		2.5 cm	
6 in	½ ft	15 cm	
12 in	1 ft	30 cm	
36 in	3 ft	1 yd	90 cm
40 in		100 cm	1 m

ENDNOTES

Chapter 1

1. U.S. Food and Drug Administration. "Use of the Term Natural on Food Labeling," Accessed January 24, 2020. https://www.fda.gov/food/food-labeling-nutrition/use-term-natural-food-labeling.

2. Oldways Whole Grains Council. "Identifying Whole Grain Products," Whole Grains 101. Accessed January 24, 2020. https://wholegrainscouncil.org/whole-grains-101/identifying-whole-grain-products.

3. Ocean Spray. "100% Juice Cranberry," 100% Juice. Accessed January 24, 2020. https://www.oceanspray.com/Products/Juices/By-Type/100-Percent-Juice/100-Percent-Juice-Cranberry.

4. Chassaing, B., et al. "Dietary Emulsifiers Impact the Mouse Gut Microbiota Promoting Colitis and Metabolic Syndrome." *Nature* 519.7541 (2015): 92–96. doi: 10.1038/nature14232.

5. Neltner, T., and M. Maffini. "Generally Recognized as Secret: Chemicals Added to Food in the United States." *Natural Resources Defense Council Report.* April 2014. Accessed January 22, 2019. https://www.nrdc.org/sites/default/files/safety-loophole-for-chemicals-in-food-report.pdf.

6. O'Callaghan, Tom F. "Nutritional Attributes of Grass-Fed Dairy," *Dairy Nutrition Forum* 11.2 (September 26, 2019). https://www.researchgate.net/publication/336059335_Nutritional_attributes_of_grass-fed_dairy.

7. Pesticide Action Network. "Pesticides on Milk," *What's on My Food?* Accessed January 24, 2020. http://www.whatsonmyfood.org/food.jsp?food=MK.

8. U.S. Department of Agriculture. "Meat and Poultry Labeling Terms," Food Labeling Fact Sheets. Accessed January 24, 2020. https://www.fsis.usda.gov/wps/portal/fsis/topics/food-safety-education/get-answers/food-safety-fact-sheets/food-labeling/meat-and-poultry-labeling-terms/meat-and-poultry-labeling-terms/.

9. U.S. Department of Agriculture. "Guidelines for Organic Certification of Poultry." Accessed January 22, 2020. https://www.ams.usda.gov/sites/default/files/media/Poultry%20-%20Guidelines.pdf.

10. U.S. Department of Agriculture. "Meat and Poultry Labeling Terms," Food Labeling Fact Sheets. Accessed January 24, 2020. https://www.fsis.usda.gov/wps/portal/fsis/topics/food-safety-education/get-answers/food-safety-fact-sheets/food-labeling/meat-and-poultry-labeling-terms/meat-and-poultry-labeling-terms/.

11. "Feeding Cattle Candy Helps Save Producers Cash." *Dairy Herd Management*, February 16, 2017. https://www.dairyherd.com/article/feeding-cattle-candy-helps-save-producers-cash.

12. U.S. Department of Agriculture. "Meat and Poultry Labeling Terms," Food Labeling Fact Sheets. Accessed January 24, 2020. https://www.fsis.usda.gov/wps/portal/fsis/topics/food-safety-education/get-answers/food-safety-fact-sheets/food-labeling/meat-and-poultry-labeling-terms/meat-and-poultry-labeling-terms/.

13. Daley, C. A., et al. "A Review of Fatty Acid Profiles and Antioxidant Content in Grass-Fed and Grain-Fed Beef." *Nutrition Journal* 9.10 (2010). https://www.ncbi.nlm.nih.gov/pmc/articles/PMC2846864/.

14. Rock, A. "How Safe Is Your Beef?," *Consumer Reports*, December 21, 2015. https://www.consumerreports.org/cro/food/how-safe-is-your-ground-beef.

15. Ibid.

16. Easton, M. D., et al. "Preliminary Examination of Contaminant Loadings in Farmed Salmon, Wild Salmon and Commercial Salmon Feed." *Chemosphere 46.7* (2002): 1053–1074. doi: 10.1016/s0045-6535(01)00136-9.

17. Pomranz, M. "Your Salmon Might Be Lying to You: Farm-Raised Salmon Isn't Naturally Pink," *Food & Wine,* March 16, 2015. https://www.foodandwine.com/news/your-salmon-might-be-lying-you-farm-raised-salmon-isn-t-naturally-pink.

18. Su, L. Y., et al. "The Relationship of Glyphosate Treatment to Sugar Metabolism in Sugarcane: New Physiological Insights." *Journal of Plant Physiology* 140.2 (1992): 168–173. doi: 10.1016/S0176-1617(11)80929-6.

19. Center for Science in the Public Interest. "CSPI Downgrades Sucralose from 'Caution' to 'Avoid': New Animal Study Indicates Cancer Risk." February 8, 2016. https://cspinet.org/new/201602081.html.

20. Malkan, S. "Aspartame: Decades of Science Point to Serious Health Risks." *U.S. Right to Know*, May 31, 2019. https://usrtk.org/sweeteners/aspartame_health_risks/.

21. Yang, Q. "Gain Weight by 'Going Diet?' Artificial Sweeteners and the Neurobiology of Sugar Cravings: Neuroscience 2010." *Yale Journal of Biology and Medicine* 83.2 (2010): 101–8. https://www.ncbi.nlm.nih.gov/pmc/articles/PMC2892765/.

22. International Agency for Research on Cancer. "Agents Classified by the IARC Monographs, Volumes 1–121." List of Classifications. Accessed January 27, 2020. http://monographs.iarc.fr/ENG/Classification/.

23. Honeycutt, Z. "Got Monsanto's Glyphosate in Your Lunch?" *Mom's Across America* (blog). https://www.momsacrossamerica.com/got_monsanto_s_glyphosate_in_your_lunch; The Alliance for Natural Health USA. "Glyphosate Levels in Breakfast Foods: What Is Safe?" April 19, 2016. https://www.anh-usa.org/wp-content/uploads/2016/04/ANHUSA-glyphosate-breakfast-study-FINAL.pdf.

24. Environmental Working Group. "Dirty Dozen Guide To Food Additives Generally Recognized As Safe – But Is It?" Accessed March 30, 2020. https://www.ewg.org/research/ewg-s-dirty-dozen-guide-food-additives/generally-recognized-as-safe-but-is-it.

25. *USA Today.* "Aquafina to Say It Comes from Same Source as Tap Water." ABC News, October 28, 2015. https://abcnews.go.com/Business/aquafina-source-tap-water/story?id=3428260.

26. Griffith-Greene, M. "Pesticide Traces in Some Tea Exceed Allowable Limits." CBC News, March 8, 2014. https://www.cbc.ca/news/canada/pesticide-traces-in-some-tea-exceed-allowable-limits-1.2564624.

27. Orci, T. "Are Tea Bags Turning Us Into Plastic?" *The Atlantic,* April 8, 2013. https://www.theatlantic.com/health/archive/2013/04/are-tea-bags-turning-us-into-plastic/274482/.

28. Kelley, G., and S. Gleason. "Common Additive May Be Why You Have Food Allergies." Michigan State University blog, *MSU Today.* https://msutoday.msu.edu/news/2016/common-additive-may-be-why-you-have-food-allergies/.

29. Kelly, S. "Teflon's Toxic Legacy: DuPont Knew for Decades It Was Contaminating Water Supplies." *Earth Island Journal* (blog). https://www.earthisland.org/journal/index.php/magazine/entry/teflons_toxic_legacy/.

30. Coyle, D. "Is Nonstick Cookware Like Teflon Safe to Use?" *Healthline,* July 13, 2017. https://www.healthline.com/nutrition/nonstick-cookware-safety.

31. Gies, E. "Substitutes for Bisphenol A Could Be More Harmful." *The New York Times,* April 18, 2011. https://www.nytimes.com/2011/04/18/business/global/18iht-rbog-plastic-18.html.

32. Earth Day Network. "Fact Sheet: How Much Disposable Plastic We Use." April 18, 2018. https://www.earthday.org/fact-sheet-how-much-disposable-plastic-we-use/.

Chapter 2

1. The Wharton School. "Not on the List? The Truth about Impulse Purchases." University of Pennsylvania blog, *Knowledge@Wharton.* https://knowledge.wharton.upenn.edu/article/not-on-the-list-the-truth-about-impulse-purchases/.

2. Gillman, M. W., et al. "Family Dinner and Diet Quality among Older Children and Adolescents." *Archives of Family Medicine* 9.3 (March 2000): 235–40. https://www.ncbi.nlm.nih.gov/pubmed/10728109.

3. Larson, N. I. et al. "Family Meals during Adolescence Are Associated with Higher Diet Quality and Healthful Meal Patterns during Young Adulthood." *Journal of the Academy of Nutrition and Dietetics* 107.9 (September 2007): 1502–1510. https://linkinghub.elsevier.com/retrieve/pii/S0002822307012928.

4. Utter, J., et al. "Family Meals and Adolescent Well-Being." *Journal of Paediatrics and Child Health* 49.11 (November 2013): 906–911. https://onlinelibrary.wiley.com/doi/abs/10.1111/jpc.12428.

5. Snow, C. E., and D. E. Beals. "Mealtime Talk That Supports Literacy Development." *New Directions for Child and Adolescent Development* (Spring 2006): 51–66. https://onlinelibrary.wiley.com/doi/pdf/10.1002/cd.155.

6. Fishel, A. "Science Says: Eat with Your Kids." *The Conversation,* January 9, 2015. https://theconversation.com/science-says-eat-with-your-kids-34573.

7. Abdel-Salam, O. M. E., et al. "Citric Acid Effects on Brain and Liver Oxidative Stress in Lipopolysaccharide-Treated Mice." *Journal of Medicinal Food* 17.5 (May 1, 2014): 588–98. https://www.ncbi.nlm.nih.gov/pmc/articles/PMC4026104/.

8. Janssens, P. L., et al. "Acute Effects of Capsaicin on Energy Expenditure and Fat Oxidation in Negative Energy Balance." *PLoS One* 8.7 (July 2, 2013). https://www.ncbi.nlm.nih.gov/pubmed/23844093.

INDEX

M

ACKNOWLEDGMENTS

To my dear daughter and favorite cooking buddy, Harley, getting to introduce new recipes and ingredients into your life has been a dream come true. You make being in the kitchen so much more fun, even if we do make a big mess. I love seeing the joy on your face when you eat something yummy that we make together.

To my always hungry husband, Finley, for being ready to try anything and give me honest feedback. I'll never forget when you taught me how to make oatmeal. Even though you tease me when you say you've been cooking longer than me, therefore you know better, I know who's the boss in the kitchen—me!

To my mother, Veena, who is the greatest cook that I know. My favorite restaurant will always be at your house. To my dad, who I love to make cake for, and who loves to eat it.

To my mother-in-law, Diane, for the beautiful ways you taught me to set a table and the importance of having gorgeous china.

To Laura for making every family get together so delicious, and for your enthusiasm for my cooking. To my father-in-law, Finley, brother Yog, Judy, Summers, and Taylor for putting up with my ingredient inquiries.

To my auntie Toni for teaching me how to entertain, and cousin Reeva for being my helper and taste tester throughout the years. To Nicole and Sandra for yummy goji drops.

To Sushila Melvani and Sri Aurobindo Society for the prayers and blessings.

To my amazing Food Babe Team—Kim and Pam, without you both this book wouldn't have happened. Your amazing contributions will continue to inspire people to eat real food for years to come. Kim, your skill to photograph food and recipe test is so impressive. Thank you for making these recipes look and taste mouthwatering.

To my agents Steve Troha and Scott Hoffman, thank you for years of amazing partnership and the love you both have for my mission.

To my Truvani Team for making the best, cleanest, organic protein powder on the market that made its way into so many of my smoothie recipes.

To Susan Stripling, the most fun photographer ever—your spunk and creativity are amazing—you have the most uncanny ability to capture the most perfect emotion in a photo.

To the entire Hay House family, thank you for your incredible support, love, and persistence to get this book out to the world. Especially to my editors Mary Norris and Sally Mason-Swaab who always put me at ease when I thought I was running out of time to get the last edits in.

To my recipe tester Sarah Tegnalia who made the most thoughtful and appetizing enhancements to this book.

To all the restaurants that inspired me throughout the years—Inn Season Café, abc kitchen, and Café Gratitude.

And most of all, thank you to my readers—The Food Babe Army—who told me early on to write this cookbook. I feel so grateful for the opportunity to create this for you and your families.

ABOUT THE AUTHOR

Named as one of the Most Influential People on the Internet by *Time* magazine, Vani Hari is the revolutionary food activist behind FoodBabe.com, co-founder of organic food brand Truvani, *New York Times* best-selling author of *The Food Babe Way* and *Feeding You Lies*. For most of her life, Vani ate whatever she wanted—candy, soda, fast food, processed food—until her typical American diet landed her where that diet typically does, in a hospital. Despite her successful career in corporate consulting, Hari decided that health had to become a priority. Her newfound goal drove her to investigate what is *really* in our food, how it is grown and what chemicals are used in its production. The more she learned, the more she changed and the better she felt.

Encouraged by her friends and family, Hari started a blog in 2011. FoodBabe .com quickly became a massive vehicle for change. She subsequently led campaigns against food giants like Kraft, Starbucks, Chick-fil-A, Subway, and General Mills that attracted more than 500,000 signatures and led to the removal of several controversial ingredients used by these companies. Through corporate activism, petitions, and social media campaigns, Hari and her Food Babe Army have become one of the most powerful populist forces in the health and food industries. Her drive to change the food system inspired the creation of her new company, Truvani, which produces real food without added chemicals, products without toxins, and labels without lies. Hari has been profiled in *The New York Times* and *The Atlantic,* and has appeared on *Good Morning America*, *CBS This Morning*, CNN, *The Dr. Oz Show*, *The Doctors*, and NPR. Vani Hari lives in Charlotte, North Carolina, with her husband, Finley, and daughter, Harley. Visit her online at: FoodBabe.com.

HAY HOUSE TITLES OF RELATED INTEREST

YOU CAN HEAL YOUR LIFE, the movie, starring Louise Hay & Friends
(available as a 1-DVD program, an expanded 2-DVD set,
and an online streaming video)
Learn more at www.hayhouse.com/louise-movie

THE SHIFT, the movie,
starring Dr. Wayne W. Dyer
(available as a 1-DVD program, an expanded 2-DVD set,
and an online streaming video)
Learn more at www.hayhouse.com/the-shift-movie

* * *

*Crazy Sexy Kitchen: 150 Plant-Empowered Recipes
to Ignite a Mouthwatering Revolution,* by Kris Carr

*Make Your Own Rules Cookbook: More Than 100 Simple,
Healthy Recipes Inspired by Family and Friends Around the World,* by Tara Stiles

The Official Bright Line Eating Cookbook: Weight Loss Made Simple,
by Susan Peirce Thompson, Ph.D.

*The Real Food Revolution: Healthy Eating, Green Groceries,
and the Return of the American Family Farm,* by Congressman Tim Ryan

*The Sugar Brain Fix: The 28-Day Plan to Quit Craving the Foods
That Are Shrinking Your Brain and Expanding Your Waistline,* by Dr. Mike Dow

All of the above are available at your local bookstore,
or may be ordered by contacting Hay House (see next page).

* * *

We hope you enjoyed this Hay House book. If you'd like to receive our online catalog featuring additional information on Hay House books and products, or if you'd like to find out more about the Hay Foundation, please contact:

Hay House, Inc., P.O. Box 5100, Carlsbad, CA 92018-5100
(760) 431-7695 or (800) 654-5126
(760) 431-6948 (fax) or (800) 650-5115 (fax)
www.hayhouse.com® • www.hayfoundation.org

———

Published in Australia by: Hay House Australia Pty. Ltd.,
18/36 Ralph St., Alexandria NSW 2015
Phone: 612-9669-4299 • *Fax:* 612-9669-4144
www.hayhouse.com.au

Published in the United Kingdom by: Hay House UK, Ltd.,
The Sixth Floor, Watson House, 54 Baker Street, London W1U 7BU
Phone: +44 (0)20 3927 7290 • *Fax:* +44 (0)20 3927 7291
www.hayhouse.co.uk

Published in India by: Hay House Publishers India,
Muskaan Complex, Plot No. 3, B-2, Vasant Kunj, New Delhi 110 070
Phone: 91-11-4176-1620 • *Fax:* 91-11-4176-1630
www.hayhouse.co.in

———

Access New Knowledge.
Anytime. Anywhere.

Learn and evolve at your own pace
with the world's leading experts.

NOTES